HOW TO MONEY

HOW TO MONEY

YOUR ULTIMATE VISUAL GUIDE TO THE BASICS OF FINANCE

Jean Chatzky, Kathryn Tuggle, and the
HerMoney team

illustrated by Nina Cosford

ROARING BROOK PRESS
NEW YORK

Published by Roaring Brook Press
Roaring Brook Press is a division of Holtzbrinck Publishing Holdings Limited Partnership
120 Broadway, New York, NY 10271 • fiercereads.com

Library of Congress Cataloging-in-Publication Data
Names: Chatzky, Jean Sherman, 1964- author.
Title: How to money : your ultimate visual guide to the basics of finance / Jean Chatzky,
    Kathryn Tuggle, and the HerMoney Team ; illustrated by Nina Cosford
Description: First edition. | New York, NY : Roaring Brook Press, [2022] | Audience: Ages
    12–18 | Audience: Grades 10–12 |
Summary: "There's no getting around it. You need to know how to manage money to know
    how to manage life—but most of us don't! This illustrated guidebook from *New York
    Times*–bestselling author and financial expert Jean Chatzky, Kathryn Tuggle, and their
    team at HerMoney breaks down the basics of money—how to earn it, manage it, and use
    it—giving you all the tools you need to take charge and be fearless with personal finance.
    How to Money will teach you the basics of: –creating a budget (and sticking to it) –scoring
    that first job (and what that paystub means) –navigating student loans (and avoiding
    student debt) –getting that first credit card (and what "credit" is) –investing like a pro (and
    why it's important!). All so you can earn more, save smart, invest wisely, borrow only when
    you have to, and enjoy everything you've got!"— Provided by publisher.
Identifiers: LCCN 2021039971 | ISBN 9781250791696 (trade paperback)
Subjects: LCSH: Money—Juvenile literature. | Finance, Personal—Juvenile literature. |
    Budgets, Personal—Juvenile literature.
Classification: LCC HG221.5 .C48 2022 | DDC 332.4—dc23
LC record available at https://lccn.loc.gov/2021039971

Our books may be purchased in bulk for promotional, educational, or business use. Please
contact your local bookseller or the Macmillan Corporate and Premium Sales Department at
(800) 221-7945 ext. 5442 or by email at MacmillanSpecialMarkets@macmillan.com.

Please note, this book is intended as a resource and offers guidance and information on
handling money and personal finance. Examples of typical situations and solutions to
common issues encountered by individuals are included for illustrative purposes only. If the
reader needs advice concerning the evaluation and management of specific legal or financial
risks or liabilities, they should seek the help of a licensed, knowledgeable professional.

Brand names included in this book are used for informational purposes only, and this book is
not authorized, endorsed, or sponsored by any owners of those brand names.

First edition, 2022
Book design by Aurora Parlagreco
Printed in the United States of America
ISBN 978-1-250-79169-6
7 9 10 8 6

For all the members of the HerMoney.com community—current and future. We do what we do every day because of you. And we are so grateful to be a part of your lives.

CONTENTS

A NOTE TO ALL OUR READERS FROM JEAN AND KATHRYN

Money isn't pink or blue; it's *green*. One of our favorite personal finance reporters, Jane Bryant Quinn, said that a long time ago, and we've held on to it for years. Why? Because it's true!

So, yes, this is the *Her*Money guide—and it's written by a team of women—but we know that many of you who picked up this book may not be. Whether you identify as nonbinary or male, we want you to know that we see you, we're here for you, the advice in this book is for you, and we're SO glad you found us! We want this book to be an inclusive read for all.

That said, as you read, you'll notice that some of the language in this book specifically elevates women, and if you read the stats on the historic gender wage gap on pages 8–9, you'll understand why. Women have long had an uphill battle when it comes to being financially empowered and respected in the workplace, and in everything we do at HerMoney.com, we're seeking to close that gap and level the playing field for financial confidence and power across all genders.

You'll also see us reference parents a few times, and we know that not everyone has a mom and dad or a family support system they can count on. And even when you have a loving parent in your life, it's no guarantee that they'll know how to manage *their* money. In fact, many of us are raised by people for whom money is a huge source of stress, because they never learned the money management basics that you're about to learn or because they suffered through financial setbacks (like a job loss or discrimination) that they couldn't control.

What we want you to know here is simple: Your financial journey is your own. You are always in control of your personal relationship with money. Some of us start with nothing. Some of us have financial help from our families. Some of us are raised by people who fear money. Some of us come from people who love crunching numbers. But we all make mistakes and face obstacles. The important thing is that we educate ourselves so the decisions we make around money can be as empowered as they possibly can be.

We're truly so excited that you're going on this journey with us and taking those first important steps toward a bright financial future. Because when you're done with this book, we know there's nothing you won't be able to tackle when it comes to your life goals and to your money.

iNTRODUCTiON
HOW To MONEY

What do you want from your life? I want you to—quickly—answer that question. Without being guarded. Without limiting yourself. Just pull the things you want most out of the air as fast as they occur to you. Make a rapid-fire list. Like . . .

A dog.
A car.
Ace my finals.
College.
A scholarship for college.
Backpack through Europe.
Experience a big love.
Go viral.
Start a business.
Run for office.
Go to grad school.
Save the planet.
Become a chef.
See Japan, South Africa, India, too.
Heck, maybe I could even live there?
Write a novel.
Run a marathon.

Be healthy.

Be happy.

Great list, right? Fun exercise? And isn't it interesting that the more time you give yourself to do it, the more expansive those goals become? College leads to med school, which leads to opening your own clinic or practice. Two weeks in Europe leads to a semester abroad, which leads to spending a few years living and working in an incredible new country.

The amazing thing is that all of these things (well, except maybe going viral; that's actually super hard) are possible. They're more than possible. What's standing in your way? Just two things: Time. And money.

Time will come. It's inevitable. The clock will continue to turn, and the months and years will pass. Money is the harder part because it doesn't automatically come your way. There are steps you have to take and things you need to do in order to earn, save, and invest money—turning it into *more* money for the future. You also have to protect the money you have so that it doesn't vanish in a flash.

And while you'll learn a lot of what you need to master life—and what it may throw at you—in school, you're probably not going to learn a whole lot about money. Maybe you'll have the opportunity. If there's an elective in personal finance, take it (please!), but chances are, it will not be a requirement. That's a huge problem. Because money is not just a tool that helps you accomplish whatever you want to accomplish in life . . . it's *the* tool.

WHAT iS MONEY, EXACTLY?

This is not just an important piece of knowledge to have; it's one of those pieces that you really want some clarity around. Why? Because if you ask a handful of people this question, you'll probably get a bunch of different answers.

The Merriam-Webster Dictionary says it's: "Something generally accepted as a medium of exchange, a measure of value, or a means of payment."

Beyoncé says it's freedom: "I felt like it was time to set up my future, so I set a goal. My goal was independence."

Some people may even try to tell you that it's "the root of all evil." *Not!* First of all, the actual verse from the Bible is: "For the love of money is the root of all evil . . ." You could take that to mean greed is evil. But even then, we'd argue that it's what you *do* with your money that's the difference between good and bad.

Confusing, right? While none of those answers are wrong, to us they don't feel complete. So let us introduce you to *our* definition. Money is *a tool*. It's *a device*. It's something we use to get us all of those things that we want in life. (See list above.) But *using* money—earning it, spending it, saving it, investing it, giving it away—is actually just one piece of the puzzle.

That's because money isn't a tool like, say, a hammer or a hair dryer. Yes, you use it to do something. It has a function. It has a job. But though you might love your hammer or you might be devoted to your hair dryer, neither one likely inspires the wide range of emotions that money does.

CHECK YOURSELF: THE EMOTION OF MONEY

Money doesn't come with an instruction manual. That's why we wrote this book and why you're reading it. But chances are pretty good that before you even flipped to page one, you were aware of some of the good-with-money basics. You know that you shouldn't spend more than you have. You know that too much credit card debt is a bad thing. You know that you should try to save. And yet, even people who know these things do the opposite. All. The. Time.

Why? Our emotions get the best of us. So do our brains. In college—maybe even in high school—you will eventually read about a famous experiment called the Marshmallow Test. A psychologist from Stanford University named Walter Mischel put children in a room with a small treat—a marshmallow, or a pretzel for kids who were anti-marshmallow—and told them if they could hold off eating it for fifteen minutes while he left the room, they could have *two* treats instead. He was testing the children's ability to wait or, as researchers say, to delay gratification. And this experiment found that kids who passed the test—who were able to wait fifteen minutes to get double the marshmallows—did better later in life. They did better in school, better on their SATs, had fewer problems with substance abuse, and they were more likely to be better with money. But why?

Versions of the Marshmallow Test hit us hundreds of times a day in our real financial lives. We're presented with things we want—to buy, to consume, to experience—all of which cost money, and we have to decide: Yes or no? Now or later? If we decide yes, our brains give us a little high-five by releasing a dose of the feel-good chemical dopamine (the same thing you get a shot of when you eat chocolate or get kissed). We like the feeling of that feel-good chemical, so our brains translate that as "spending money = good." Except, for

our long-term financial futures, spending money is not always so good. We need to be able to control ourselves. That means being able to distinguish between things we need (food, air, water, warmth) and things we want (pretty much everything else).

STRESS? YES. :(

Another big reason why we have to control our spending and make good judgment calls about our money is stress. You've probably experienced stress many times, like before a big test or when a friend was mad at you. We all have stress in our lives, and sometimes there's absolutely no way to prevent it. But one thing to realize early about money is that it can bring on a huge amount of stress—particularly not having enough of it when you need it, feeling like you're not in control of the money you have, or allowing yourself to compare your financial situation too often with the people around you (more on this in a sec).

The truth is that financial worry—if you don't learn how to control it—can be incredibly dangerous. People who have higher levels of debt have higher levels of depression, and when you're stressed about money, you're more likely to suffer physical problems such as headaches, sleepless nights, and even high blood pressure.

The solution is to learn to a) recognize it, and b) deal with it. When we first feel money stress creep into our lives, our instinct might be to avoid addressing the problem, but this becomes a vicious cycle because when we ignore our money (by not paying a bill or not checking our account balance), it often makes the issues worse. When, instead, we take control of our finances and gain an understanding of how our money works, we can eliminate our fear of the unknown and become more confident with our money than ever before.

BALANCE: The amount of money you have in a bank or brokerage account at a particular time.

Knowledge really *is* power when it comes to our money, and this is true no matter how much you earn. In fact, when you don't earn much, that's even more of a reason to up your money game and learn how to make it work for you, all of which we can't wait to share in the coming chapters.

SWiPE UP

We all compare ourselves to others, even if we don't always realize it. On Insta. And Snapchat. And TikTok. And every other social media platform where we can scroll and admire all day long and sometimes late into the night. The average teen spends 7 hours and 22 minutes on their phones each day. (This doesn't count schoolwork or time spent listening to music or reading books.)

But what are you doing when you're on these platforms? You're swiping through new videos, pictures, and stories from the people you follow—people who likely include celebrities and other influencers. You're liking, of course, but you're also comparing, which often leads to *wanting*.

Have you ever seen a friend or a stranger online with a new back-pack, phone, or whatever and thought: *I have to get that*? or *I like that so much better than the one I have*? And then you dwell on it for a while. Or maybe you buy it, right then and there, this thing that you didn't know you even wanted but suddenly had to have? That was your emotion getting the better of you—and your money.

FAiR? NOT REALLY.

Those comparisons—and the fact that social media can convince us that having more money means having more power, more popularity, more love (or at least more likes)—are just one way that money makes its way into every single one of your relationships. Not just the ones with your family, your friends, your significant others, your coworkers, and your classmates, but also the ones with society and the world.

Later in this book we're going to talk about earning money (aka income), because earning money is a very good thing. Earning *more* money is even better. Because when you

Social media platforms are also designed specifically to get you to spend more money. Instagram, for example, has countless ads and in-app buying, and on all platforms your behavior is being tracked so companies can find more effective ways to make you spend. Even though social media can be a wonderful way for you to join social justice movements, keep in touch with family, and never miss a friend's birthday, don't lose sight of the fact that you're being enticed to spend, spend, spend with every tiny heart you offer.

are a good earner, you can use your money to create the change that you want to see in the world. You can donate your time and money to causes you care about, and you can watch as your contributions elevate your fellow women, save animals, or make countless other impacts. You can also invest in companies that are creating social and environmental change, enabling you to quite literally save the world—or you can even start your own company. Oh, and BTW you can reduce the stress in your own life, because being a good earner translates into being able to live a comfortable life. We're going to give you lots of ways to do that in these pages.

But before you start your career and start earning a salary, you should know that there are a lot of inequities when it comes to both race and gender. During your career, you can work to change these (one day you'll be in a position to hire people, give raises, and decide how your company is run), and you can also donate your time and money to causes that are on the frontlines working toward a better tomorrow for all. Here's a rundown of a few important terms that you may have heard before. Once you understand them, you can be part of the solution.

- **Income inequality** refers to how income is unevenly distributed through a population—or put another way, some people make much more than others. Right now in the US, the top 1% of earners make twenty times what the average earner does.
- Income inequality leads to **wealth inequality**. Income is what you earn, but your wealth (sometimes referred to as your **assets** or **net worth**) is what you have. When you earn more over a long period of time, you're able to save more and invest more.

- The **gender wage gap** is what we call the fact that women as a group earn much less than men as a group. Right now, women earn just 81 cents on average for every dollar that a man earns. For many non-white women, the gap is bigger. Black women are paid just 63 cents for every dollar a white, non-Hispanic man earns; Latinas are paid 55 cents; Native American women are paid 60 cents; and Asian American women are paid 87 cents. After they transition, trans women see their incomes *fall* by up to a third.

Throughout this book, you'll see that we use the terms "wage gap" and "pay gap" interchangeably. When you earn a paycheck from a job, you're earning a wage. So, "wage gap" and "pay gap" mean the exact same thing, but we wanted you to understand both terms so you'll know them when you hear them.

- The racial wealth gap is even more complex to explain and understand. From the inception of the United States, there have been a series of unjust, discriminatory policies designed to disenfranchise and disadvantage African Americans. Beginning with slavery, many events combined to prevent Black people from accumulating wealth in America, including the theft of millions of dollars in assets from former enslaved peoples by an institution called the Freedman's Bank; the passage of Jim Crow laws, which enforced segregation; the 1921 massacre of Tulsa's Greenwood District; and redlining that limited the ability to borrow money to buy homes in Black neighborhoods. As of 2019, on average, white families in America have wealth eight times greater than Black families.
- And, although we don't have as many statistics on this yet, there are **gaps based on sexuality** as well. Lesbian women make 12% less than straight women. Same-sex married couples have $20,000 less saved for their future retirement than heterosexual ones.
- Women with disabilities working full-time, year-round are typically paid just 80 cents when compared to their male counterparts with disabilities.

Let's just put it out there right now: This is all very, very wrong. To truly close these gaps once and for all, we'll need the combined help of society, corporations, and government policies. But there are steps you can take—yes, you!—to start closing your own gaps. And from there, you can be a part of the solution for your friends, your community, and the world at large.

LOOK AT YOU TAKING A STEP!

Learning "How to Money" is one of those steps. It's a really important one, actually. And look—you're doing that!

Here's some more good news: The financial life of someone your age is—in a good way—simpler than that of an independent adult. If you can learn the skills you need to manage your life today, you can build on them through the years so when it's time to go to college, rent your own apartment, buy your own car, etc., you can handle those things without the stress of a beginner.

And the even *better* news is that moneying like a pro is really just a matter of doing the same things over and over from now until . . . well, forever, but because you're reading this book now, you've already got a leg up. Because even though money *can* be intimidating, it doesn't have to be . . . and it won't be for you after you read this book! In the next fourteen chapters, you're going to learn "How to Money." For simplicity's sake, we've broken those chapters into five parts.

Part 1: Earn It. Here's a big #lifetruth. It's harder to care about something if you aren't involved with it. You care more about a class when you're taking it and more about managing money when you have some. This section is all about access to money. We'll talk you through how to earn it yourself and how to handle the money you receive in the form of an allowance or gifts.

Part 2: Manage It. Once you have money, you want to make smart

decisions when it comes to saving it, spending it, and investing it. Part of that process is being thoughtful about your money, so we'll dive into how to a) set goals, and b) make them happen. We'll talk budgeting, accounts, and apps that can help you keep this growing financial world of yours together.

Part 3: Use It. Of course, we'll talk about spending. Your money is a limited resource, so you want to use it like a boss! That means getting good deals (on everything), knowing the difference between new and used (and why used is better for you and the planet), and starting to think about those first mega expenses, including your first car and your first apartment.

Part 4: Get Schooled. There's no doubt that getting an education pays off. But these days, it's more important than ever to consider the value of a college education and to seriously consider student loan debt before you take it. We'll take a look at different careers, what they pay, and how to navigate toward them.

Part 5: Look to the Future. Finally, we'll wrap up by talking about your health and your money and break down how learning about your money helps you stress less. Because we want you to be happy. *Really* happy. Learning how to use your money in a way that lines up with your values will give you that happiness boost.

BUT WAIT, THERE'S MORE

Along the way—in every one of these parts—we'll equip you with tactical advice and information. We're talking tips, exercises, definitions ('cause you have to know the lingo), infographics, and more. Plus, you'll meet some amazing, really cool women who will inspire you to up your money game.

Most excitingly, we think you'll very quickly see—as we have—that money is fun. Knowing "How to Money" makes you feel powerful and independent and really, really smart. Yes, you're all of those things already. But who wouldn't want to be just a little bit more? As we say at HerMoney.com: We got you.

xoxo,

Jean, Kathryn, and the HerMoney team

PART 1

EARN IT

1

LET'S GET TO WORK

You Can't Really Learn to Manage Money until You Get Some

Somewhere along the way, someone—someone older, let's be honest—said to you: Time is money. And maybe you thought: *Yeah, okay*. But it's actually a really important concept.

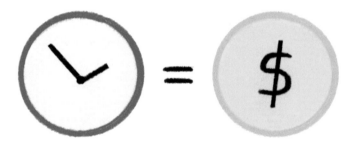

Here's the deal: You have twenty-four hours in a day. Eight (at least!) should be for sleeping. Another eight-ish are for school or a combo platter of school-and-studying. This leaves you with around eight hours of freedom in your day. See how quickly that time flew? Like 💨. That's why time is one of your most precious resources.

Money is another one. And while the amount of money you can make is somewhat limited (particularly when you're young), it's less limited than time. If you put your mind to it, you can make more.

Throughout your life, you'll work, which essentially involves trading time for money. You do a job. The job takes time. You get paid for putting in that time. (There are other instances where you can make money in your sleep—by investing money you've already earned, for example—but we'll get to those later.)

So let's look back at those eight free hours. What are you going to do with them? Maybe you want to make some money. This is how we start to place a value on time. The middle-of-the-night hours aren't super valuable to you right now (you need those ZZZZs). But those after-school hours when you're not studying? Those weekends? Those are yours to do with as you wish. You can hang with your friends, sure. However, if you make the decision that you'd like to put some money in your wallet, you can also trade them for cash by working.

SOME TiME iS MORE VALUABLE THAN OTHER TiME

When you take your first econ class, one of the initial lessons you'll learn will be the relationship between supply and demand. You'll see a graph that looks like the one below. Supply and demand move in opposite directions, and where they overlap, that's the price.

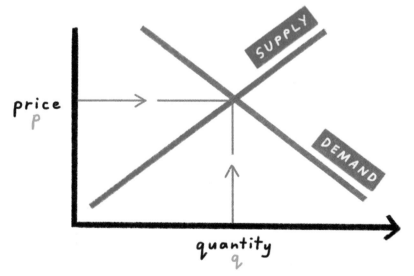

Think of toilet paper at the beginning of the coronavirus pandemic. People were really afraid that we were going to run out, so they started buying up—hoarding, really—toilet paper. They demanded more. That behavior led to a shortage of toilet paper, driving the supply down. Stores like Costco had to limit purchases to one pack at a time. And the price? Because demand was much greater than supply, it skyrocketed. Later on, when people realized they didn't need to hoard as much and there was going to be enough to go around, demand returned to normal levels. The toilet paper supply stabilized (there was plenty on the shelves), and the prices went back down.

Your time is a little like toilet paper. It's more valuable when there's more demand for it. Let's take the holidays, for example. If you work at a retail store, you might get paid more than normal for working the early hours on Black Friday, when the store needs a ton of help. Then it's up to you to decide what is more important to you—a few more hours of shut-eye or the extra cash in your paycheck. When you get out into the working world full time, you'll also see that there are times when jobs are really plentiful and others when the pickings are slim. When they're plentiful, you'll likely get paid more because there are more jobs than workers who want them. When they're slim, employers can ask you to do more for less.

The value you place on your time and your money can also help guide you in career choices. If you're focused on making a lot of money, you might enter a career in finance or become a doctor. Both fields are traditionally laden with long hours but also with high paychecks. If you're someone who prefers a flexible schedule and plenty of time to yourself, you might have to sacrifice some of that pay for more hours in the day. Maybe you'll become a college professor and have time off between semesters, or a freelance graphic designer and make your own schedule. Neither is right or wrong; it just matters what matters to you. (We'll talk more about your career choices and your money in chapter 12.)

HEY, NO FAiR! WHY DOES HE MAKE MORE FOR THE SAME WORK?

"We do a disservice to our country as a whole when we don't value people equitably."—Katica Roy, *gender economist, founder and CEO of Pipeline Equity.*

To understand the gender pay gap—the fact that women, on average, still earn only 81 cents for every dollar a man earns, and women of color earn even less—you have to flash back to World War II. Men went to war. Women kept the factories running by going to work. But there was no law in place to ensure that women were going to be paid the same as the men were—so they weren't.

Once the men returned and the war was over, plenty of women realized they enjoyed working and wanted to stay in the workforce. The men got their jobs back at higher salaries. The women who stayed were paid less. Was it fair? Of course not. Not then and not now. Even though women are making 81 cents on the dollar, they are not paying 81 cents on the dollar for, say, a gallon of milk. But because there was no precedent for women in the workforce, the situation didn't get a lot of pushback.

Even today—when there *is* a lot of pushback—the gap isn't closing very quickly. A study from the American Association of University Women says it won't actually *be* closed until 2119. Yes, a century from now. And the fact that millions of women lost jobs or left the workplace during the pandemic to care for their families may put us back another twenty years. Clearly, that won't do. So how can you help close it for society and make sure that you are paid fairly for the work you do?

- **Elect Leaders Who Want to See the Gap Closed.** Vice President Kamala Harris wants to bring back a policy that requires companies with one-hundred-plus employees to publicly disclose pay based on gender and race. This helps because it forces companies to be transparent about pay, effectively shaming them into leveling the playing field. Plus, this federal law would fine all companies not paying equally for equal work. But it's important not just to approach this on a federal level. Get to know your elected officials—members of Congress, governors, mayors, city councilmembers—and let your voice be heard. You can create change. If you don't like how something is being done, speak out, organize, and don't give up until you see positive change being made.
- **Know What Fair Pay Is—and Ask for It.** Women traditionally have not negotiated for pay as much as men have. That's changing, but it's also still a problem we have to solve one at a time. Whenever you go for a job—whether it's a dog-walking gig, a job in a store, or for a company—do some online research to figure out what the going rate is in your area. Then ask for it. Say: "Based on my experience and the going rate for this sort of work, I am expecting to be paid $15 an hour." (Or whatever the rate is.)
- **Talk to Your Friends about Pay.** Let's just put this out there: Talking about how much money you make isn't rude, and it isn't mean; it's helpful. Because when you share, you are letting others know what's possible—and helping them understand if they're being treated unfairly. Speak up.

READY, SET, WORK!

So you want to make some money? Great! There are plenty of opportunities, no matter how old you are, but they fall into a few basic categories. First, there are the informal jobs like babysitting, pet walking, lawn mowing, etc. These are jobs or tasks that neighbors or other people pay you for directly, usually with cash or Venmo.

Then there are the more formal ones, where you typically fill out a job application and you get an actual paycheck. For the latter, working at a retail store or a nearby restaurant, you'll need to have working papers (more on that in a sec).

Finally, there are the entrepreneurial ones, where you essentially make your own job by starting your own business. You might set up an Etsy store, selling anything from makeup to T-shirts to laptop stickers. Creativity is the only barrier to entry. For example, after purchasing stick-on nails for her own use, thirteen-year-old Joelle Hinds decided she could do them better. She ordered plain press-ons and started painting them herself, creating a library of colors and designs that she sells at her Etsy storefront.

How much you can make will vary by your age, your area, and your experience. For the informal jobs, like babysitting, the going rate in the area determines what you get paid. For the formal ones, you'll make at least the minimum wage. This is the dollar amount most official employees have to make per hour no matter what. While the federal minimum wage is set at $7.25, a lot of states have set their minimum wages significantly higher.

You can get an informal job as soon as you can find someone to hire you. (Most of us at HerMoney started babysitting and doing other jobs around age eleven.) But before you can get a formal job, you need to know: Am I eligible to work? Each state has a law about how old you have to be to get a job—in most, age fifteen is the minimum. Next, you'll need something called **working papers**, which you'll get through the Department of Labor in your state or from your employer. A parent or guardian will need to sign them if you're under eighteen.

LOTS OF JOBS OVER YOUR LIFETIME

The advice you'll read over the next few pages is designed to take you from the very first job you have as a teenager into the **internships** you'll have

in high school and college and maybe even that first real job. Remember, as you get your first job, it'll be one of many, many, many, *many* that you will hold over the course of your life. Most of today's adults have held twelve over their careers, on average.

> **INTERNSHIP:** Work done by a student or trainee, sometimes without pay, in order to gain work experience or earn college credit.

Think of these jobs as rungs on a ladder. That babysitting gig might lead to a job in a store, which might lead to an internship (or three), which will lead to a real job. For the first job, you won't write a resume. You may not even have an interview. But as your jobs get more formal, more professional, you'll have both. You'll write cover letters. You'll have not just a single interview for a position, but several. You

may even be asked to complete a case study or take a test. (Yes, they want homework before you even get the job.) You're not there yet—but over time, you will be—so we're going to give you the 411 on all of the building blocks you'll need.

For right now though . . . chill. It's okay that the first job you hold is in no way your dream job. It's even okay that it's not at your dream company. While you think a big name might look best on a resume, think again. At a small company, you'll likely be given more responsibility, like working on major projects that are typically above your rank when a team needs extra help. You'll have experiences with higher-ups that will teach you more than you ever expected.

And job title and company are not the only factors in accepting a position. Salary and benefits (like health insurance, paid vacation time, and a retirement account like a 401(k)) matter, too. All of these combined are called your total compensation, or total comp for short. This can and should be a factor in whether or not you decide to take a job. There may even be, as you enter the realm of internships, some people or companies who want you to work for no pay. (These are called unpaid internships.) You should know they're not legal unless you get college credit. Even then, getting paid is better. But if it's a great experience and you need to satisfy an internship requirement to graduate, you may do it. And that's okay, too.

TIME TO APPLY

A job isn't going to fall into your lap. Well, sometimes it does if someone you know needs help, and you volunteer that you're available and would like to do it. (This doesn't happen often, so step up when it does!) Most of the time, you'll have to go job hunting. That means searching online and off for positions that align with your interests and experiences. Each posting comes with an application—a form to fill out with your personal information as well as professional history. Many ask for a resume and cover letter as well.

What are these? A resume (pronounced re-zuh-may) is a one-page doc that outlines your education, work experience, and other accomplishments and skills. A cover letter is basically a written introduction to you and your resume. Some jobs will ask for one, others won't. But when you do write one, it should explain a little bit about why you're applying for this particular job, and why you think you'd be a great fit.

Here are some pointers to keep in mind when drafting your resume:

- Don't use a boring template. Have a little (though not too much) fun by using a free service like Canva. Pick out a clean but interesting template, and copy and paste the information you need to include.
- If you don't have experience because this is your first job, put education at the top instead.
- Don't be afraid to let your personality shine!
- If you're a writer, an artist, or have work you'd like to exhibit, build a portfolio online and link to it on the resume.

And here's what a resume might look like. This is actually the real resume that Rebecca Cohen (who helped write this book) used while she was in college. It landed her an internship at theSkimm (!) and eventually a job at HerMoney.com.

BUILD A PORTFOLIO TO
SHARE YOUR WORK

REBECCA COHEN

CONTACT

E: MailBag@hermoney.com
P: (555) 555-5555
W: rebeccamcohen.com
123 Main Street
Small Town, New Jersey

SKILLS & ABILITIES

COMPUTER PROGRAMS
Microsoft Office
Photoshop
Bridge
Premiere Pro
InDesign
Audition
GarageBand
iMovie
iTunes
Parse.ly
CrowdTangle
Banjo

SOCIAL MEDIA
Twitter
Instagram
Facebook
Snapchat
LinkedIn

LANGUAGES
Proficient in Spanish

ACTIVITES

ALPHA EPSILON PHI SORORITY
Alpha Mu Chapter
Vice President of Standards
December 2016 - December 2017

SOCIAL

@beccamcohen

@becca_cohen

EDUCATION

EXPECTED BA IN JOURNALISM, MINOR IN CREATIVE WRITING
University of Maryland College Park | August 2015 - May 2019
GPA: 3.63

MEDIA EXPERIENCE

FREELANCE REPORTER
The Hollywood Reporter | September 2017 - Present

- Write news and feature stories on live entertainment events as they are happening. Cover large events such as the American Music Awards and the Golden Globes in present time while writing and publishing stories about the event on assignment.

SOCIAL JOURNALIST AND AUDIENCE ENGAGEMENT EDITOR
Capital News Service | August 2018 - December 2018

- Managed social media accounts and webpage for the news organization, create social content and editorial content for the social media accounts and website, analyze and report analytics and engagement information.

EDITORIAL INTERN
Baltimore STYLE Magazine | January 2018 - May 2018

- Editorial intern for lifestyle magazine in Baltimore. Covered lifestyle events and cultural happenings in the Baltimore area working both from the office and on assignment.

ONLINE EDITORIAL INTERN
The Hollywood Reporter | June 2017 - August 2017

- Wrote news and feature stories focusing on the entertainment industry and related news. Stories range from breaking news for immediate publish to long-term feature and listicle projects for later publication. Coverage of carpet and other events for various movies, television shows, and Broadway shows including on-site interviews, transcription, and write-ups for same day publication.

STAFF WRITER
Unwind Magazine | March 2017 - January 2018

- Wrote compelling lifestyle stories on a range of topics for a prestigious, student-run, lifestyle and entertainment-based magazine. Stories are published either online, in print, or both and reach thousands of UMD students campus-wide. Gathered content for stories by interviewing subjects and doing research based on the topic.

WORK EXPERIENCE

COUNSELOR AND GROUP LEADER
Camp Wayne for Girls | Summer 2016 and Summer 2018

- Led campers to activities and cared for one bunk of campers for seven weeks at sleepaway camp.

INTERN
The Writing Center at UMD | August 2016 - January 2017

- Edited and revised papers and other writing assignments for students in need. Worked six hours per week.

CLEAN BUT
INTERESTING
TEMPLATE

LET YOUR PERSONALITY SHINE!

Next up, we have a cover letter Rebecca used to apply for an internship. Each cover letter should be tailored to the job you're applying for. And, like Rebecca's does, it should have a first sentence or two that makes you really want to read more.

REBECCA COHEN

New Jersey / Maryland | (555) 555-5555 | MailBag@hermoney.com | rebeccamcohen.com

October 16, 2018
NBC Washington
4001 Nebraska Ave. NW
Washington, D.C. 20016
Dear NBC Washington Recruiting Team:

START WiTH AN ATTENTiON GRABBER.

Picture this: It's lunchtime rush hour in NYC and I got a cab with barely enough time to make it to my interview. In record-setting time, I scarfed down my cold Grubhub grilled cheese as I approached my destination. With seconds to go, I took a swig of water too quickly, the open bottle landing in my lap leaving me looking like I had just peed in my pants. Disheveled and embarrassed, I was ushered to a fancy suite where I waited to interview TV directors Billy Ray and Chris Keyser. As an intern, I was sure I was about to make a fool of myself in front of these accomplished men. Instead, I rode the misfortune like a wave and joked about my stain when I entered the room. We shared a laugh and continued to have a productive and nerve-free conversation about their Amazon TV Series, *The Last Tycoon*.

News writing and reporting are my main journalistic interests, with a focus on feature writing and political, entertainment and lifestyle news. In the summer of 2016, I had hands-on experience while working under the Senior Online Editor at *The Hollywood Reporter* (THR.com). I wrote stories varying from breaking news to evergreen pieces focused on long-term entertainment, or even political, trends. At THR.com, I also channeled stories onto different platforms so each story could reach its appropriate niche audience. Currently, I freelance for THR.com by reporting news breakouts on deadline from large entertainment events such as the Golden Globes and the AMAs.

EXPLAIN WHO YOU ARE AND WHY YOU'RE APPLYiN

Right now, I work as a social media editor and data journalist for Capital News Service Maryland, a student-run wire service committed to producing news for our Maryland audience. I create compelling social content daily, strategize where that content goes across multiple social platforms, and compile an analytics report for my team weekly. I am looking to further my education in this part of the field and become more immersed in all things digital.

As an intern at NBC Washington, I am confident I will be able to handle the fast-paced and unique news reporting environment, thanks to my rigorous reporting training in both my classes and previous and current internship experiences. In my news writing and reporting course, I was required to write two news pieces weekly on my assigned beat, and in my feature writing course, I juggled interviews with multiple story assignments on varying topics. In the Spring, I travelled to Baltimore, Maryland once weekly to *Baltimore Style Magazine* in addition to a full course schedule.

This opportunity intrigues me because of my intense commitment to following and reporting breaking news stories daily as well as working on the digital side of news. Working in this special newsroom would be my perfect fit due to my upbeat and eager personality. I would love to have the opportunity to contribute alongside seasoned reporters whose work ethic and professionalism I admire deeply.

FOCUS ON WHY THE RECRUiTER SHOULD HiRE YOU.

Thank you so much for your time in considering my application. I look forward to hearing from you soon.

Sincerely,

Rebecca Cohen

MAKE SURE TO PROOFREAD!

Always remember:

- Do not use a cover letter to just regurgitate your resume. It should be different and share new information.
- Start with an attention grabber. Let them know you're excited about their company and the role they have available. (Yes, this means each cover letter you write should be tailored to the specific role you're applying to!)
- Include a short paragraph *quickly* explaining who you are, what you've done in the past, and why you're here.
- Focus on why the recruiter should hire you: This is how I can fix your problem, this is how I can help, and this is what I am going to do in this role (with examples).
- Lastly, proofread, proofread, proofread. A typo or grammatical error can quickly make a hiring manager move your application to the bottom of the stack (or worse, the garbage can). Triple-check everything before you send it out.

NAiLiNG AN iNTERViEW: iT'S ALL ABOUT THE FiRST iMPRESSiON

Here are seven things you need to know to crush any job interview:

1. **Dress for the Job You Want.** This means understanding how people dress to work where you're applying (if it's a store, just walk in), then copying it. Even if the company is pretty casual, it never hurts to take it up a notch.
2. **Come Prepared.** Bring a copy of your resume with you. And don't let the conversation surprise you. Do research on the company, the interviewer, and the industry.

Knowing enough to answer the question "Why do you want to work here?" with specific examples is a good start.

3. **Show Some Initiative.** Is the position at the local newspaper? Show up with a typed list of ten story ideas you'd pitch as a writer. Are you hoping to intern at an aerospace engineering firm? Show off that jet you built for class last semester by including a link to photos of your project.

4. **Act Like a Pro . . . But Not a Know-It-All.**
When you get hit with a question you're not sure how to answer, don't panic. Instead, take a beat, consider what you know about the company, combine that with your personal experience, and doctor up something that works. A lot of the time, interviewers aren't looking for the perfect answer—they just want to see the logic you follow in getting to one. BTW: A bear can run faster than an alligator. (Yes, they actually ask that question.)

BREATHE

5. **R-E-S-P-E-C-T.** An interview is a chance to prove you're someone the team would like to work with. Showing off your manners and maturity are half—maybe even more than half—of the battle. Even if you feel silly, hold the door open, shake hands, say "please" and "thank you," and smile until your cheeks hurt.

6. **Ask Good Questions.** Yes, an interview is where you have to answer questions, but at some point, the interviewer will likely say, "Do you have any questions?" And you need to say yes. Here are some options that always work, no matter the position. Pick a couple to go with.

    – *What can I expect out of a normal day?*
    – If you're speaking to the hiring manager: *What do you like most about your role?* If you're speaking to HR: *What do you like most about working at this company?*

- *What is the most difficult part of this job?*
- *How did you get involved with this industry/company?*
- *What will my main responsibilities be in this job?*
- *How does someone succeed in this company?*
- *Are there opportunities for growth on the team? If so, what are they and what does the timeline look like?*
- *What skills will I need to use on a day-to-day basis?*
- *What is the team missing and how can I fill that role?*
- *What should I expect from the rest of the interview process?*
- *May I have a business card?*

    You want to make sure you have their contact info when you walk out the door so you can thank them and follow up as needed.

7. **Follow Up.** After any interview, circle back to say thanks with a quick email. (Seriously. We know people who didn't get a job because they didn't send one.) Ideally, you'll do this within twenty-four hours of meeting with them. Include a gracious "thank you for your time," a reminder of something you discussed, and an explanation of how excited you are about the opportunity. Do not expect an answer. But if you haven't heard back from the interviewer or a recruiter in the promised timeframe, feel free to follow up with another quick and courteous email.

YOU GOT THE JOB, CONGRATULATIONS! NOW WHAT?

Now it's time to prove you're up to task and will be the best employee they've ever hired, just like you promised in your interview. The time you roll into the office says way more about you than you'd think, and it all comes down to your actions showcasing how much you care. Let us give you two scenarios:

- Intern A is supposed to arrive by 9:00 a.m. She's at her desk by 8:45, scrolling through last night's emails, saying "good morning" to other early arrivers, and sipping the coffee she made in the office kitchen. By the time her manager arrives at 9:05, she's caught up and ready to get to work on the next project.
- Intern B scrambles through the door at 9:15 a.m.—iced coffee in tow—and has to face her boss, who has been there for ten intern-less minutes already. She still has to take time to catch up on last night's missed details before launching into today's project, which is now delayed by at least thirty minutes.

Need we say more?

Okay, fine. We're not all Intern A *all* the time. We have our Intern B days, and that's fine, as long as you don't make every day an Intern B day. Arriving early and being (mostly) honest about when you start working are two factors under a larger, more ambiguous umbrella of being professional. That means clearly communicating what you're working on, trying hard to build relationships with the people you're working with, and even signaling that you're having a problem with something you've been asked to do well before you were supposed to finish it.

PAY EXPLAINER: HEY, WHERE DID MY MONEY GO?

We're really sorry to be the ones to tell you this. When you get your first real paycheck, you may notice some money missing. Yes, missing. If this is a full-time job, some of the money might have been deducted to help pay for your health insurance or fund your 401(k). (Don't worry, we'll get to what this is in a minute.) Even generous companies now ask employees to help split the cost of these items. But the rest of the missing money? That's taxes. All employees are required to give a portion of your hard-earned money back to the government in taxes.

Here's how taxes work. Every **pay cycle**, a portion of your paycheck will be automatically deducted and sent to the government—the federal one, but often the state and local ones, too. This is called **withholding**. The money that is withheld in taxes pays for things like government programs, including Social Security and Medicare, which you will benefit from in retirement.

Now, let's break this down a bit further and show you what this looks like. Assuming . . .

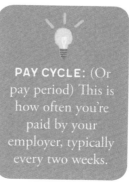

- You're an Illinois resident
- Making a $52,000 annual salary ($1,000 per week)
- Falling in 2020's tax brackets as a single filer (which means you're a single person with no spouse or children)

PAY CYCLE: (Or pay period) This is how often you're paid by your employer, typically every two weeks.

You'll see withheld:

- Federal Tax: 22% or $220 per week ($440 per pay cycle)
- State Tax: 4.95% or $49.50 per week ($99 per pay cycle)
- Social Security: 6.2% or $62 per week ($124 per pay cycle)
- Medicare: 1.45% or $14.50 per week ($29 per pay cycle)

Now let's see this all in action . . .

PAYCHECK
Pay period: Jan. 20 - Feb. 2

Employee Name
123 Main St.
City, USA

EMPLOYEE EARNINGS

Description	Rate	Hours	Current	Year to Date
Regular Hours	$50	40	$2,000	$6,000

EMPLOYEE TAXES WITHHELD

Employee Tax	Current	Year to Date
Federal Income Tax	$100	$300
Social Security	$100	$300
Medicare	$20	$60
State Income Tax	$25	$75

FICA/
PAYROLL
TAXES

EMPLOYEE CONTRIBUTIONS

Description	Current	Year to Date
401 (K)	$50	$150

SUMMARY

EX. 401(K)

Gross Earnings	$2,000
Pre-Tax Deductions/Contributions	$50
Post-Tax Deductions/Contributions	$0
Taxes	$245
Net Pay	$1,705

THIS IS THE AMOUNT YOU GET TO TAKE HOME!

THIS IS THE TOTAL AMOUNT YOU MAKE,
BEFORE WITHOLDING AND DEDUCTIONS.

TAX BASICS

Federal Income Tax: Federal income taxes provide the largest source of income for the federal government—that's why you are constantly hearing them being debated in Congress. In general, Democrats believe in bigger government programs and support as well as higher income taxes, while Republicans believe in fewer programs and support as well as lower income taxes. Federal income taxes are used for everything from infrastructure (building roads and bridges, for example) to education, public transportation, and disaster relief.

State Income Tax: These are taxes on income you earn either working in the state or working for the state. While most states have income taxes, nine states—Alaska, Florida, Nevada, New Hampshire, South Dakota, Tennessee, Texas, Washington, and Wyoming—don't. Sometimes people move to these states for that reason. State income taxes pay for state and local programs.

Payroll Taxes aka FICA (Federal Insurance Contributions Act): The third type of taxes taken out of your paycheck are payroll taxes (though you may see them listed as **FICA**). These pay for Social Security and Medicare, two big government programs. Social Security taxes provide retirement and disability benefits for employees and their dependents. Medicare taxes provide government health insurance for people sixty-five and older as well as some younger people with disabilities. Your employer chips in for these taxes, too.

We know what you're thinking. "You mean out of my $2,000, biweekly paycheck, I'm only taking home $1,258?" Um, yes. But don't panic. In your early years, when you're likely only working part time, even if all these taxes are taken out, you'll likely get a lot of that money back. How? Let us introduce you to a little thing called tax refunds.

When Tax Day rolls around each year (usually April 15), workers who earned more than $12,200 (in 2021) have to file a tax return. If you didn't make that much and taxes were taken out of your paycheck, you can file a return, and the money will be given back to you, otherwise known as a "tax refund." If you made that much or more, filing a tax return is essentially how you settle up. If too much money was taken out of your paycheck based on your income, you'll get a refund. If too little was taken out, you'll have to write a check to the government to pay them what you owe. P.S., If you have earnings of your own (and want to claim your refund), you have to go through this process if you're still a dependent—a child under nineteen or a student under twenty-four. In that case, your parents get tax breaks for your care and feeding as well.

401(K): WHAT iT is AND WHY iT's iMPORTANT

If you're reading this book straight through, you may have noticed a couple of times now that we've referenced something called a 401(k) as a way to save for retirement. We know that's a *very* long way off for you, but since you'll likely start saving in one of these accounts in your twenties, we wanted you to have all the details.

A 401(k) is a retirement savings account that you open through your employer, and your employer often adds money called matching dollars to it on your behalf . . . for free! As soon as you have a job that offers one of these plans, you'll want to sign up for it immediately because if you don't, you're literally leaving free money on the table.

Here's how it works: If you earn $40,000 per year and you decide to save 6% of your salary, that means you're taking $2,400 directly out of your paychecks and putting it into your 401(k). But if you have an employer who matches 50% of your contributions, the company will put an additional $1,200 into your 401(k) as an incentive to get you to save. This is why sometimes people refer to their 401(k) as a place to get free money. It really is! All you have to do is take the first step to save, and then your company will kick in their contribution. Later on, when it's time for retirement, you'll have even more money waiting for you. It's a no-brainer!

We can't wait for you to open your first account—"future you" will thank you!

DEAR BLACK GIRL: WHAT i WOULD SAY TO MY TEENAGE SELF ABOUT THE RACiAL WEALTH GAP

By Javacia Harris Bowser

My teenage self never thought she could be a homeowner, and that's a truth that breaks my heart.

Even though my parents worked very hard and made sure my younger brother and I never went hungry, many bills went unpaid. They could never afford to buy a house. Year after year, we moved from one rental home to the next. So, my teenage self was convinced that home ownership was only for rich, white folks—and as a Black girl from a family quite familiar with the phrase "insufficient funds," that certainly didn't include me.

I wish I could go back in time to tell teen me she deserves a home of her own and anything else she wants in life.

But I wouldn't sugarcoat the facts. I'd be honest and say, *Yes, the odds are stacked against you, and when you're all grown up, the numbers will still be discouraging.*

The gender pay gap is real. The racial wealth gap is real, too. You already know this, but the ever-evolving statistics regarding gender and racial inequities bear repeating. As I'm writing this, women earn just 81 cents on average for every dollar that a man earns. For women of color, the gap is even wider. Black women are paid just 63 cents for every dollar a white, non-Hispanic man earns; Native American women are paid 60 cents; and Latinas are paid 55 cents. White families in America, on average, have wealth eight times greater than Black families. Slavery, decades of discrimination, Jim Crow laws (which forced segregation), and redlining (which limited the ability to borrow money to buy homes in Black neighborhoods) have all contributed to the systemic racism that threatens to hold back Black people—especially Black women. If your parents have had every door slammed in their faces, how can they open a window of opportunity for you?

But you are stronger than statistics. That's what I would tell my teenage self, and that's what I'm telling you.

Learn as much as you can about money. This book you're holding in your hands is a great start. But don't stop with this. I wish my teenage self would have had access to the websites, resources, and social media platforms created by millennial money experts like Tonya Rapley of My Fab Finance and Dasha Kennedy of The Broke Black Girl. I wish she could have been able to learn from nationally recognized financial educator Tiffany Aliche of The Budgetnista.

Get your money management in check right now. Look at the money you have coming in—whether that's from an allowance, a part-time job, or a scholarship—and assess how much money you have going out. Track your spending to figure out where you need to cut back. (Are *all* of those Target trips really necessary?)

Create a budget and stick with it. After you've covered any bills you have to pay, allot some money for fun, but also set aside money for savings. When you're tempted to blow up your budget, think about your future self and the life you want her to have. In fact, make a vision board or try journaling about the life of your dreams. Describe the life you want as if it's already yours, and read this whenever you need encouragement to make smart money moves.

I finally became a homeowner six years ago. My husband and I bought a three-bedroom, two-bathroom house and I love everything about it from the high ceilings to the hardwood floors.

Don't let anyone or anything dim the light of your dreams.

TL;DR

CHAPTER 1 KEY TAKEAWAYS

- You're going to have lots of jobs over the course of your career. Think of your progression through the working world as a ladder that you're climbing to the top.
- When you look for a job, you should try to find one with the best possible salary, but also consider what it's like to work there and what the benefits are, like a 401(k) retirement plan or health benefits. You have to evaluate the total package.
- Having a good resume and cover letter are so important when it comes to landing a good job. Your application materials should be tailored to each job, typo-free, and make the hiring manager want to read more.
- After you interview for a job, follow-up is key. Make sure you send an email or handwritten note to thank the interviewer for their time.
- When you get your first paycheck, take time to bask in the glow of earning money. You did it! But be prepared to have money taken out for things like taxes and retirement contributions.

CLAIRE WASSERMAN

FOUNDER AND CEO OF LADIES GET PAID

WHICH WORDS DEFINE YOU?

Resilient, creative, empathetic, optimistic, enterprising, communicator.

WHAT'S YOUR JOB?

I'm the founder of Ladies Get Paid, a platform and community that helps women level up professionally and financially. I'm also the author of *Ladies Get Paid*, the book, which is all about how women can take command of their careers to earn what they're worth.

WHAT'S THE CHANGE YOU'RE LOOKING TO CREATE IN THE WORLD?

I want for women to achieve equity with men, both in terms of power and pay. Part of that is learning to empower ourselves, but the other part is improving our company policies as well as our governmental policies so that all women may rise.

TELL US ABOUT YOUR FIRST JOB.

My first job after graduating was as a development associate for Chess in the Schools, a nonprofit that uses chess as a way to get lower income kids excited about education and on a path to college. I was paid $37,000 and that was in 2009.

WHAT'S THE BIGGEST MONEY MISTAKE YOU EVER MADE?

Not learning about it! The second worst mistake was going into thousands of dollars of credit card debt. I didn't realize how high the interest was.

WHAT'S THE SMARTEST MONEY MOVE YOU EVER MADE?

Realizing that it's less about how much money you make and more about how much of it you spend.

TELL US A MONEY STORY THAT MADE YOU WHO YOU ARE TODAY.

After graduating college, I moved to New York with $300 in my bank account. My generous cousin let me crash on his couch for six months. I lived off of chickpeas and cans of tuna, and eventually I saved enough that I could move into my own place.

WHAT ONE PIECE OF CAREER ADVICE WOULD YOU GIVE TO YOUR YOUNGER SELF?

Don't be so hard on yourself! I think that pushing myself was, in some ways, a good motivator, but I've come to realize that you don't need to be so hard on yourself to achieve great things. In fact, you'll probably get there a lot sooner if you take time to really slow down and let yourself be truly proud of yourself.

WHAT ONE PIECE OF MONEY ADVICE WOULD YOU GIVE TO YOUR YOUNGER SELF?

Invest! Just a little bit goes a long way over time. Plus we can't let men make all the money. :)

WHAT ARE THE TOP THREE THINGS EVERY TEEN NEEDS TO KNOW ABOUT GETTING PAID?

1. Do something that makes you come alive. If there's a skill that comes naturally to you and/or a job that gives you energy, go in that direction.

2. You are your best advocate. Don't assume your hard work is going to be recognized. Learn how to embrace and articulate your value, which includes (always) negotiating your salary.

3. Know your values. Being clear about your values will make it easier to know what decisions to make and what paths to pursue.

2

STARTING YOUR OWN BUSINESS

There Are So Many Ways to Turn Your Free Time into Money-Making Opportunities

HOW DO YOU START A BUSINESS?

Google started in a dorm room. Amazon started in a garage. Apple was started by two college dropouts. Now they're the biggest companies in the world. Businesses have interesting life stories, just like you or me.

If you're itching to create a new product or service you feel is needed in the market, go for it. But understand that starting a business and being self-employed means something very different today than it did just a decade or so ago. Thanks to the internet and social media, to be an entrepreneur, you don't have to open a physical store or even work typical hours. You could open an Etsy store; run a thriving business as a freelancer by finding clients to pay you for your skills (writing, photography, or graphic design, for example); or operate as a gig worker, doing tasks for other people (usually finding work via apps) and getting paid for them. Uber drivers are gig workers, for example, but so are many people who do home-repair projects or rent out their homes via Airbnb.

> **FREELANCER:** Someone who makes money by finding clients to pay them for skills they have in a particular field.

Whichever way you go, do some research first by asking yourself these questions:

- What do I want to create?
- Is it a product or service?
- Do products or services similar to mine already exist?
- If so, what are they?
- How is my product or service different/better?
- If it's not that different/better, why do I think the world needs more?
- What are other similar products or services charging?
- How much money/time will it cost me to get started?
- Who are potential customers, and how do I reach them?
- How much time do I have to keep this going?

By answering these questions, you are basically creating an informal business plan—a set of information that lays out what you want to do and how you're going to do it. It doesn't need to be super formal. But it is smart to gather these details before you get started—even if what you're trying to launch is a part-time side hustle.

Diane Mulcahy, author of *The Gig Economy*, recommends experimenting with your product or service before launching. Figure out how to create or offer it to a handful of people you think might be interested before you start marketing it to many. For example, if you're looking to go into business screen printing T-shirts, and you know you want to sell to people your age, then your friends are the perfect audience to help you get started. What do they think of your designs? Do they like the material of the shirts and the variety of sizes? How much would they be willing to pay per shirt? They can help you work out the kinks.

Another great way to gain insights is to volunteer for a little while. Consider it research. Are you thinking about offering your social media services? Head to the local animal shelter and offer to run their Instagram feed for a few months. Are you looking to sell your amazing granola to stores in your community? Offer to provide a few bags for free to get feedback and see if it's popular.

Once you figure out what's working and what isn't working, refer back to your initial plan and tweak it. In the words of the great Ross Gellar: pivot, pivot! Your product, service, marketing plan, and even your goals need to be flexible enough to be changed as you learn more about yourself and your business. Very few entrepreneurs get it right on the first try.

Another thing to think about: Cold. Hard. Cash. You need to have a good handle on how much money you need in order to make some of your own. This is called capital. For example, how much will it cost to make a bag of that granola? And how much time? Only once you have the answer to both questions can you figure out what to sell it for. You should also realize that it may be a while before you start making any money at all. How much are you willing to put into this business in order to get there? And where is that money going to come from?

FINDING CUSTOMERS

When you're ready to launch, you need to find people to buy your product or service. These are called customers or clients. You can go old school, posting flyers in your neighborhood and asking friends to spread the word. (The good news about these efforts is that they're cheap, if not free.) But you can also go digital. Use a platform like Etsy or eBay to sell your products, or use Upwork or Fiverr to promote your services. This is the easiest (and cheapest) way to spread your message wide.

OH, YOU WANT TO BE AN INFLUENCER?

Really, who doesn't? When you're posting on social anyway, wouldn't it be nice to get paid for it?

It may be possible, but it's a lot of work and not as glamorous as it sounds. Take Instagram, for example. Many **influencers** make most of their money from sponsorships. Brands hire them to promote their products. That sounds great until you're forced to promote a product you don't believe in . . .

Also, early on, when a brand "pays" you to promote their products, they may do it with products rather than real money. And while it's nice to get a new bikini or a fancy nail polish, you can't use those items to pay for dinner or rent.

Another thing to consider? Being an influencer can be a huge time commitment, and sometimes it's really, really nice to just disconnect and not worry about putting your best face forward.

ALL IN ALL, BUSINESS OWNER . . .

Starting a business is hard work. That doesn't mean you shouldn't go for it. If your entrepreneurial synapses are firing, you should—but manage your own expectations. Know that it likely won't pay off immediately, but it will be fulfilling in the long run and is a great learning experience no matter how it turns out. Be sure to be careful, be deliberate, and be persistent. You'll get there.

TL;DR

CHAPTER 2 KEY TAKEAWAYS

- There are all kinds of ways to become an entrepreneur these days. You can be a business owner with employees, a gig worker, a freelancer, or an independent contractor. The title doesn't matter as much as deciding what kind of business you want to run.
- Before you start your business, you can get experience and test the market by volunteering, by offering your services or product for free, and by approaching your friends and family to ask for their guidance and advice.
- Here are two questions you need answers to before you launch: How much money will it cost to make this product? And how much time will it take? Only then can you decide how to price it.

MINDA HARTS

FOUNDER AND CEO OF THE MEMO LLC AND AUTHOR OF
*THE MEMO: WHAT WOMEN OF COLOR NEED TO KNOW
TO SECURE A SEAT AT THE TABLE*

WHICH WORDS DEFINE YOU?

Resilient, generous, courageous, empathetic, driven, flexible.

WHAT'S YOUR JOB?

I am an author and CEO. I help catalyze equity for women of color in the workplace.

WHAT'S THE CHANGE YOU'RE LOOKING TO CREATE IN THE WORLD?

Making the workplace better for women who feel like they are in the margins. All women don't experience the workplace the same, and I want to contribute to a world that values and humanizes the experiences of all women in the workplace. My life's work is to make sure I am providing resources to help sustain lasting change.

TELL US ABOUT YOUR FIRST JOB.

My first job was as an administrative assistant at a Fortune 500 company. It wasn't my dream job, but it was the job that I found, and it allowed me to sustain myself while living in Chicago, Illinois. At first, they offered me $28,000 a year. I knew that I needed at least $30,000 a year to cover my expenses and have a little leftover. I had no idea what salary negotiation was, I just knew that I couldn't pay all of my bills for $28,000, so I asked for $30,000. I ended up getting it. And if I knew what I know now about negotiation, I would have asked for more!

WHAT'S THE BIGGEST MONEY MISTAKE YOU EVER MADE?

Just being grateful for the salary that was presented to me. There have been times in my career when I didn't negotiate because I was just happy to have an opportunity. I had to realize that I am the asset.

WHAT'S THE SMARTEST MONEY MOVE YOU EVER MADE?

Making sure I share my salary negotiation stories with other women. The more of us who are making smarter money moves, the more it benefits all of us.

TELL US A MONEY STORY THAT MADE YOU WHO YOU ARE TODAY.

I have always been philanthropic. Every dollar I make, I give a percentage of it back to causes that I care about. Being able to be generous is a privilege.

WHAT ONE PIECE OF CAREER ADVICE WOULD YOU GIVE TO YOUR YOUNGER SELF?

You are your best advocate. Nobody is going to be able to advocate better than you for you.

WHAT ONE PIECE OF MONEY ADVICE WOULD YOU GIVE TO YOUR YOUNGER SELF?

Start saving early. I thought I had plenty of time to contribute, and I didn't start until almost ten years after college. Start investing in your future right now!

WHAT ARE THE TOP THREE THINGS EVERY TEEN NEEDS TO KNOW ABOUT STARTING A BUSINESS?

1. Understand your why; it's important to get clarity on why you want to start a business. Is this because it's your dream or someone else's?

2. Be your first investor. I saved my money in order to invest in my own company. I always thought I needed someone else before I could start, and I was able to get started by investing in myself. It wasn't a lot, but it allowed me to take my first step.

3. Work on starting solutions that make the world better for someone else.

3

THE A TO Z OF ALLOWANCE

From Asking for One to How to Use It Best

Even if you don't have a job or start a business, money will likely find its way into your hands as teens. It can come as an allowance or in the form of gifts. We'll get into managing it wisely in part 2. But for now, just a few words about those revenue sources . . .

WHAT'S AN ALLOWANCE?

An allowance is an amount of money given, usually at regular intervals, for a specific purpose. Some teens have to work for the money, some don't. It really depends on the house you live in.

But experts say the real purpose of an allowance is to teach budgeting. This works when an allowance comes regularly, like a paycheck, and when you're expected to use it to cover certain items that your parents aren't going to pay for. If you've been trying

to convince your parents to start an allowance, this is the conversation you should have:

- Start by explaining that you want to learn to handle a small amount of money now so that when you head to college or work and get a job with a real paycheck, you'll be able to manage it better. Come up with a list of items they pay for today that you could cover with your allowance. Agree that you are no longer going to ask them to pay for these things. That may be entertainment or food when you're out with friends. Gifts for your BFFs. Maybe some self-care.
- Tell your parents that your goal is to actually save them money by teaching you how to budget with a small allowance instead of having to bail you out later. (Chances are, they've heard that horror story from more than one friend.)
- Decide if you're going to offer work in exchange. Take a good look at the activities on your schedule—school-related and not—and decide how many hours a week you could offer. You'll be most successful here if you offer to take on jobs that your parents do themselves or pay others to do (i.e., not ones they've already asked you to do) like laundry, walking the dog, or being responsible for the recycling. Be realistic. It's better to take on a smaller workload at first and succeed than to bite off too much and have to take a step back.
- Come prepared with a sense of the going rate. If they push back, don't cave immediately. This is your first chance to try your hand at negotiating, or trying to talk someone into giving you more than they originally wanted to. Try something like: "I spoke to five others in my class. They are receiving $X per week."
- Suggest they talk to other parents in the

neighborhood if they want confirmation of the going rate and ask when you can revisit the topic again.

If you feel you need a raise in your allowance, you should have a version of the same conversation. The best advice we can give you—and this goes for any negotiation you have during your life—is to think about it from your parents' perspective. The conversation should not be about what *you* are getting. Rather, you should tell them what *they* are getting. Even if the answer isn't "an empty dishwasher at 9:00 p.m. each night" but "a kid who isn't going to spend more than they have and then ask for more," that's incredibly valuable.

TAKE THESE SKILLS TO COLLEGE

If you're going off to college, you're going to need to have another version of this conversation. Even if you're living in a dorm and are on a meal plan, you will be spending money. You'll spend money on books, social activities, and yes, food, when the dining hall is closed for the evening. Where is that money going to come from? Will you use the money you earned from your summer job? Will you need to find a job on campus? Will your parents help you? And if so, with how much? Here's what you should consider:

- What will have to be paid for? Food? Social activities? Clothing? Books? Transportation? Travel home? If you're bringing a car to campus, gas and parking? Many colleges and universities publish sample budgets on their websites.
- How, tactically, will you manage your money? Will you

use your bank account from home? Will you open a bank account on campus? Will the bank account come with a debit card?

- Will your parents give you a credit card for emergencies? (If they want to do this, suggest they make you an authorized user. This means you would get a card with your name on it and a separate credit limit. It can also help you build credit. More on this on page 103.)

EXTRA PAY FOR EXTRA WORK

Once you've agreed with your parents on an allowance, understand that you might still have additional earning power. At HerMoney, we believe all teens should work. Why? Because only when you work do you really make the connection between an hour of your time and a sum of money. When someone gives you money—either as an allowance or as a gift—you don't get the same feeling of power and accomplishment as you do when you earn it yourself.

So where do you start? At home. There may be instances when your parents are willing to pay you to do things they would pay others to do. Yes, there's yardwork and washing the car, but get creative. If you are better than your parents at technology, offer to digitize their CDs and make playlists, to teach them how to set up the lighting for their Zoom calls, or to help them with their social media. If you can cook or grocery shop, take that on. In terms of pricing your services, find out what pros are charging for the same work and come in a little lower because you don't have as much experience. Then treat it like an actual job. Deadlines are deadlines!

TL;DR

CHAPTER 3 KEY TAKEAWAYS

- You may get an allowance from your parents—and chores, or work you do around the house, may be involved. If your parents haven't raised the idea of one, you can bring it up.
- If you're not offered an allowance, you can propose taking on jobs at home that they would pay others to do.
- The skills you learn by making your allowance last until you get paid again can help you budget in the future.

CRYSTAL ECHO HAWK

FOUNDER AND CEO OF ILLUMINATIVE

WHICH WORDS DEFINE YOU?

Hardworking, passionate, deliberate.

WHAT'S YOUR JOB?

I'm the founder and executive director of IllumiNative, the Native-led non-profit dedicated to increasing the visibility of—and challenging the negative narrative about—Native Nations and peoples in American society.

WHAT'S THE CHANGE YOU'RE LOOKING TO CREATE IN THE WORLD?

My goal is to dispel the inaccurate portrayals of Native peoples in media, entertainment, pop culture, and education. I aim to increase the visibility of Native peoples and issues, to drive the negative narrative of Native Americans toward one that is asset-driven, and to showcase our resiliency.

TELL US ABOUT YOUR FIRST JOB.

I worked as a loan secretary in a small, rural bank. It was one of the few jobs in town, but I took it as I needed to support my family.

WHAT'S THE BIGGEST MONEY MISTAKE YOU EVER MADE?

Not saving money, especially when I had big contracts and other big money opportunities come in.

WHAT'S THE SMARTEST MONEY MOVE YOU EVER MADE?

To pay down debt.

TELL US A MONEY STORY THAT MADE YOU WHO YOU ARE TODAY.

As I get older, the things I used to spend money on when I was younger aren't important or satisfying to me. Spending money on my family, community, experiences that create quality time with my daughter, self-care, and reinvestment in my well-being is money well spent.

WHAT ONE PIECE OF CAREER ADVICE WOULD YOU GIVE TO YOUR YOUNGER SELF?

Believe in yourself and your instincts.

WHAT ONE PIECE OF MONEY ADVICE WOULD YOU GIVE TO YOUR YOUNGER SELF?

Save your money.

WHAT ARE YOUR TOP THREE TIPS FOR NEGOTIATING IN ANY SITUATION?

1. Listen.

2. Ensure that everyone feels seen and heard.

3. Imperfect action is better than no action in most instances, especially when it comes to challenges facing your community.

PART 1 EXERCISES

You're already through the first part of the book! Go you! What you'll see at the end of each part are two to three exercises that help you capture what you've learned. Consider them reinforcement! Do 'em now if you like—or save them for later.

Home/Work. Want to earn money at home? Take a look around and see what needs to be done. What are some recurring (or annoying) tasks that Mom and Dad never seem to want to do? Research how much they cost when you hire someone to do them. That way you'll have an idea of what to charge.

Plan Ahead: Consider Your First Internship. You may want to intern somewhere close to home before you start college or while you're home from college during the summers. Make a list of the majors you might want to study in school or the jobs you might want to pursue. Then talk to the adults in your life and ask them about good companies that may be in your field. Make a list of the ones you might want to work for, then do your own research, starting with Google.

Getting Down to Business. If starting a business is on your to-do list, you'll eventually want to get tactical and practical. Consider: What would you do? What would you make or create? How would you market your product or service? Answer these questions to help you get started.

- What product or service would your business provide?

- Why is there a need for your product or service? How do you know?

- How would you market or promote your product or service?

- Who would your main customers be?

- How many hours each week are you able to work on your business?

- What would you want to name your business?

- How much money do you think it might cost to get your business off the ground?

- What excites you the most about this business?

PART 2

MANAGE IT

SET YOUR GOALS

The Only Way to Get What You Want Is to Know What You Want

Any time you make a decision in life that involves money, you should always try to know what you want going in—in other words, have a goal—and have a road map for achieving those goals. But what are goals, exactly? They're just the things that we want from our lives that, in many cases, we need money to help us achieve. We'll talk about how to set goals in a minute, but before we can talk about the things we want, we have to talk about the things we need.

NEEDS VS. WANTS: AKA MUST-HAVE VS. NICE-TO-HAVE

The concept of needs versus wants is probably one you already understand and make decisions about every day without even realizing it. We all have our basic survival needs, such as food, water, clothing, and a place to live. Likewise, we all have wants like that funky beaded curtain you've been eyeing on Etsy, concert tickets, or that extra side of fries. Wants are pretty much anything you'd like to have but could realistically live without. When we make decisions for how to use our money, we are essentially prioritizing those needs and wants.

NEEDS　　　　　**WANTS**

Although the concept of a need versus a want may sound simple (of course I *need* a place to live, but I *want* that new eye shadow palette), it's the foundation of any solid financial plan. You succeed when you put your needs first and limit yourself to acquiring the wants when you have the resources to truly afford them. Sounds pretty simple, but IRL it can be anything but.

THE CHOICES WE MAKE EVERY DAY

Every choice we make with our dollars should have a reason behind it. Sometimes it's easy. If you're hungry, you buy food. If you're cold, you buy a sweatshirt. Those are examples of immediate financial decisions—decisions based on what you feel is best for you in the moment.

But other times, you make decisions on behalf of future you—the person you'll be in a few months or even years. Maybe you've had the experience of being out at dinner with friends, and you consider ordering an appetizer and a dessert, but you decide to stick with just an entree so you have money left to spend on a new book that's coming out from your favorite author next month. The older we get, the bigger the purchases you—and future you—want (and need) to make, the more complicated these decisions become.

Why? We live in a world of instant gratification. Virtually anything we want can be ordered with a couple of taps on our phone screen then delivered right to our door. The temptation is very, very real. But even though spending on smaller treats for ourselves can feel really good (hello, dopamine), reaching our big financial goals feels even better.

Think about it this way: You've probably already had the experience of working hard toward a big goal. Maybe you tried out for a sports team, a debate team, a band, or a dance squad. You invested hours into memorizing routines, learning the rules of the game, or practicing the notes. Now think how good it felt when you finally achieved your goal and were offered a spot. It was probably much more exciting and impactful than, say, acing an easy pop quiz, right?

Those smaller things you spend money on—like dinners out or new clothes—those are the easy vocab tests. Sure, they're nice to have, but they aren't really going to change your life. Those bigger things we invest our money in—like a car or a college education—those are the coveted spots on the team, the big life goals we can really be proud of. You need those big goals because having them makes bypassing the small purchases easier. You know *why* you're doing it. Learning to wait now (remember the Marshmallow Test?) will set future you up for success later in life.

MAKING THE HARD CHOICES EASIER

Easier isn't the same as easy, unfortunately. So here's one way to sort through any decision you're facing. Make a good old-fashioned pro/con list.

Maybe this is something you've done before—you'll start by drawing a line down the middle of a sheet of paper, creating two columns. In one column, you'll have the pros (the positives), and in the other column you'll put the cons (the negatives). For example, if you're trying to decide between spending the money you saved on a spring break trip versus buying a car, your list might look a little something like this:

PROS	CONS
TIME SPENT WITH FRIENDS	WILL SET MY SAVINGS GOAL BACK BY $1,000
RELAXING ON THE BEACH	WON'T HAVE CAR BY FOOTBALL SEASON
SEE A NEW CITY / MAKE NEW MEMORIES	MUST KEEP RIDING BUS FOR 6 MORE MONTHS

Your list can be as long or as short as you want to make it; the goal is that you put thought into each thing you write down and consider how it will impact your life positively or negatively. And while making this list may only take you ten minutes, the time you spend with it should be much greater. Sit with your list for a few days. Try not to do anything (or spend anything!) for a week, and see how your priorities change.

BITE-SIZED SUCCESSES

A goal, as we said, is something, anything you want to accomplish in life. The bigger the goal, the longer it typically takes and the more important it is to break it down into smaller, more manageable pieces. Why? Because when we can experience small successes along the way, we're more likely to stick with the process. We're more likely to make it to the big goal at the end. But if we can't see that we're getting there, we're more likely to give up.

Part of this is because we need time to accomplish our bigger goals. For example, if you want to buy a used car that costs $5,000, you simply *can't* go out and buy it tomorrow. You'll need to save $100 a month (or whatever you can afford to save) over time in order to buy your car in a couple of years. So your overall goal is still that $5,000, but your monthly goal is just $100 or about $3 per day. In this way, all our bigger goals are comprised of smaller, more manageable goals. Whenever we look at a big goal's smaller pieces, it makes it easier for our brains to manage and comprehend.

When I Save...

$500 ⟶ Dinner!

$1,000 ⟶ Jeans!

Don't discount how important tracking your path to your goal is. When we're just starting, big goals seem insurmountable. But when we celebrate each step toward the accomplishment we make, then the journey can be so much more enjoyable—even fun!

HOW TO SET—AND REACH—ANY GOAL

If you're ready to achieve a savings goal, here's how you do it:

1. Name your goal and put a price tag on it.
2. Decide when you want to achieve it.
3. Do the math: Divide the time and money between now and your goal into those bite-sized pieces. These are called benchmarks.

For example:

You want to save for a weekend trip with your friends. It costs $400. The trip is three months from now.

Do the math: $400/3 months = $133/month or $33.25 a week.

Save that much every week by moving the money automatically from your checking account to your savings account. (More on automation in the next section!) Or, if you don't have an account, put that much in a drawer or other hiding place that you aren't tempted to raid.

TRICKING OURSELVES INTO SAVING

For all the reasons we've been talking about, saving money for a far-away goal—putting future you ahead of the wants you have today—is tough. When we see money come into our bank account, and we've worked hard for that money, the temptation to "treat yo' self" is very, very real.

This is why sometimes we have to "trick" ourselves into saving more. What does that mean, exactly? It may mean rewarding ourselves for hitting certain goals—for example, if you save $100, you can use $10 for a small splurge. But it can also mean removing the obstacles in our way so that we don't have to think about it. For example, if every single month you have to log into your bank account and transfer $100 from your checking account into your savings account, there's a good chance that you'll forget—or spend that money before you can save it. This is why we **automate**. Check it out.

ultimate in automation because the money comes right out of your paycheck. You don't see it. You don't touch it. You don't spend it. Presto.

THE HABIT is THE THING

So how much money do you need to start working toward your goals? As much as you have. Seriously, you can start with as little as $1! Identifying your goal and putting aside that first bit of money is taking a big step. The next is to lay out a plan for when you'll be able to put away the next dollar and the dollar after that.

The ultimate goal is to build a lifetime habit of saving. And that means building good habits overall.

HOW TO BUILD GOOD HABITS OVER A LIFETIME

Have you ever heard that it's easier for little kids to absorb foreign languages or to become bilingual? It's kind of the same concept with habit building—the earlier you start, the easier it is. "Our brains are more 'plastic' when we're younger, so it's much easier to start building good habits at this early stage," says Katina Mountanos, author of *On Adulting* and a clinical psychologist. "Your brains are better able to build those positive pathways." Here are three habit-building hacks:

1. Get into a routine—slowly. For example, if you want to get into the habit of making your bed, don't tell yourself

that it has to be done every single day, no matter what. Instead, set a goal to make your bed three days a week and see how that feels. Mountanos calls these microhabits, and with them, the goal is to pay attention to the smaller steps you're taking every day, which will one day have a broader ripple effect in your life.

2. Pair a job with a pleasure. You might not like taking money out of your wallet and putting it in the bank every month (or even transferring it on Venmo), but if on the same day you treat yourself to your favorite smoothie, then you'll start to have a positive association with this financial chore. "It's all about perspective," Mountanos says. "If you view these things in a way that is exciting, it becomes easier and easier over time."

3. Accept mistakes and move on. If you get off course with a habit that you're trying to build, don't beat yourself up. "When we make a mistake, our brains are conditioned to react in a way that says, 'I did something bad; nothing will ever be good again,' but that's not true," she says. Whenever you find yourself slacking, try to view it as part of the learning process—you'll do better next time!

TL;DR

CHAPTER 4 KEY TAKEAWAYS

- Some goals in life require money to achieve them. Having a plan or road map can help us succeed in getting there.
- It sounds basic—but knowing the difference between something you need versus something you want will be key throughout your life.
- Breaking down your bigger financial goals into smaller, bite-sized pieces called benchmarks is a big help. For example, if you want to save $1,000, you can't do it all at once! Instead, try saving $20 fifty times or save $50 twenty times.
- We can trick ourselves into saving more money by giving ourselves little rewards along the way and by using technology to move our money into a place where we're less likely to spend it.

ViCKi ROBiN

CO-AUTHOR OF *YOUR MONEY OR YOUR LIFE* AND PIONEER OF THE FIRE MOVEMENT

WHICH WORDS DEFINE YOU?

Funny, inquisitive, articulate, deep thinker.

WHAT'S YOUR JOB?

I am a social change agent and a writer, which means I think, wonder, notice, synthesize, risk, and hope to move people with my words.

WHAT'S THE CHANGE YOU'RE LOOKING TO CREATE IN THE WORLD?

To teach people practical ways to live well together within the ecological means of the earth.

TELL US ABOUT YOUR FIRST JOB.

I worked at the 1963 World's Fair for a day, earned a dollar an hour, and then got fired. After that, I was a waitress in New York City.

WHAT'S THE BIGGEST MONEY MISTAKE YOU EVER MADE?

I believe my hyper-frugality—while clever and nobly dedicated to keeping my ecological footprint tiny—distorted my choices and, at times, diminished my self-care.

WHAT'S THE SMARTEST MONEY MOVE YOU EVER MADE?

I've lucked out three times now in buying houses at the bottom of the market and building wealth.

TELL US A MONEY STORY THAT MADE YOU WHO YOU ARE TODAY.

Life only starts making sense when you serve a purpose greater than yourself.

WHAT ONE PIECE OF CAREER ADVICE WOULD YOU GIVE TO YOUR YOUNGER SELF?

Find a range of people you respect and who see the good in you, and ask them to help you find what you are good at, what you would do even if no one paid you, and what impact you want to have in the world. Then ask them to help you try on some roles in society through internships, education, networks, and introductions.

WHAT ONE PIECE OF MONEY ADVICE WOULD YOU GIVE TO YOUR YOUNGER SELF?

While fame and fortune are not the point, being wildly successful professionally doesn't have to mean you are selling out, selling your soul, or compromising your values. Be a little less pure and a little more bold.

WHAT ARE THREE WAYS THAT MONEY AND HAPPINESS ARE INEXTRICABLY LINKED?

1. Having steady income liberates your creativity, courage, talents, and opportunities for learning.

2. You buy leisure, and with time, you can let your life find its natural course in the great river of humanity.

3. If you learn to be generous with your surplus, it can produce a feeling of great satisfaction that you can help others.

HOW TO BUDGET

The Pathway to Making Your Money Work for You

We talked a lot about the importance of having goals in chapter 4. Budgeting is the next step in this conversation. So what is a budget? In short, it's a plan that outlines how you're going to use (in other words, spend and save) your money to reach those goals.

Maybe you've never heard the word *budget*. But here's the thing—if you've ever spent money, you've already had experience budgeting.

Say you have $100 to spend on back-to-school clothes. You know that you can buy five $20 items ... one $50 item plus two $25 items ... or three $30 items plus one $10 item. You've done this kind of math in your head countless times. Any time you find yourself thinking, *How much can I spend now, and how much will I need to save for later?*, guess what? You're budgeting.

Easy, right?

So why, then, do only 47% of Americans have a budget? Many were never taught how to manage their finances. (You won't have that problem. We've got you.) Others feel budgets are like diets—they're restrictive. We disagree. We think budgets are freeing. They help us prioritize and better use our money. They give us a framework that we can use to make choices rather than just going through life spending without thinking about it. And they help us reach our goals.

SO WHAT GOES INTO A BUDGET?

An adult budget has four main parts: needs, savings/debt, wants, and charity. Yours may not be as complicated or contain all of these just yet, but it's helpful to look ahead and see where each category fits in.

NEEDS

Housing: Rent (or when you buy a home, a mortgage payment) plus the cost to live there like taxes and maintenance.

Transportation: Public transportation or the cost of your car (including gas, parking, and insurance), bike, or whatever you use to get around.

Groceries: Food purchases in a grocery store. (Note: Eating out is different—it's a want.)

Utilities: Internet, power, gas, cable, etc.

Health care: Insurance, prescriptions, and doctor bills.

Household supplies: Toothpaste, dish soap, laundry detergent, etc.

Cell phone bill: The amount you spend on your phone and data plan every month. Note: While having a phone to keep in touch is definitely a need, getting a new phone every time one launches is a want.

Clothing: The clothing that you need to stay warm, keep cool, or look professional at work are absolutely needs. But your third pair of black booties bought "just in case" should walk themselves right on over to the wants category.

SAVINGS / DEBT

Savings: The money you put into your emergency account, retirement account, or brokerage/investment accounts. Aim to save 15% of whatever you have.

Debt: Student loans, credit card bills, and any other money you owe that you need to pay off.

WANTS

Personal: Salons, products. All nice but with few exceptions (yes, there are times you need a haircut), they are not needs.

Fun: Restaurants, games, music, movies, vacations, streaming services, and anything else you'd like to have but could live without.

CHARITY / DONATIONS

This is the money you want to donate or use to give back to your community in some way. The only item in this category but an important one!

TRACKiNG YOUR SPENDiNG iS THE SECRET TO BUDGETiNG

So, as we said, a budget is a *plan*—more specifically it's a dollar-by-dollar spending-and-saving plan for all the money you have. But it's really hard to make one if you don't know where your money is going now. That's why tracking your spending is the secret sauce to building a budget that works. In other words, you should do this *first*.

What does it mean to track your money? It's pretty simple, really—it means keeping a list (on paper, on your computer, or on an app) of what's going in and what's going out. This information will give you a framework to evaluate—and then modify—your choices. Once you see that you're spending $30 on birthday gifts for each of your friends, you can decide that sounds like too much and try to spend $20 instead (or to chip in with another friend and each spend $15 on that $30 gift). This information gives you power over your money.

Here's a handy list of credits (payments) and debits (expenses). It can help you see areas where you might be able to cut back and save money. Or where you might choose to use your money differently. And remember how, in the last chapter, we talked about the habit of saving? Here you see it in action. Every time this budgeter gets money, she moves 15% of it to savings. (Once you have a regular, predictable paycheck, you can move that money automatically.)

CREDITS: Payments that are credited to your bank account like your earnings from a paycheck, a birthday check from Grandma, or any other deposit you make.

➕	1/10/2022	$50 Credit—Babysitting Money
		$7.50 Transfer to Savings (Because You Should Always Save 15%)
➖	1/15/2022	$6 Debit—Takeout
➖	1/18/2022	$27 Debit—Amazon
➖	1/21/2022	$32 Debit—Venmo to Jules
➕	1/23/2022	$100 Credit—Birthday Money
		$15 Transfer to Savings (Again, It's 15%)
➕	1/27/2022	$300 Credit—Biweekly Pay from Part-Time Job at the Bookstore
		$45 Transfer to Savings (You guessed it—15%)
➖	1/29/2022	$14 Debit—Gas
➖	1/30/2022	$30 Debit—Share of Cell Phone Bill to Mom and Dad

WHAT'S UP WITH 15%?

One of the questions we get asked *a lot* at HerMoney is: How much do I need to save for the future? The answer is 15%. That's the amount that research has proven works best. If you can save 15% consistently over your working life, which generally lasts from your twenties into your (gulp) late-sixties, it will give you enough to live comfortably for the rest of your life. You won't just put that money into savings—you'll invest it so that it grows (we'll talk about that in chapter 8), but saving enough is the key. If you don't save enough, you won't have money to grow.

What if you *just can't* save that much? Don't be intimidated. You can start by saving just 1% or 2% of what you earn. Over time, as you get a job that pays you more money or get a raise, you can increase your contributions. And if you want to save more than 15%? Be our guest. Many people do, and as a result, they can stop working sooner. Or, when they hit periods in their life when they can't save as much, they don't have as much stress.

Finally—one happy hack to keep you inspired? Visit your savings. Wherever you keep them, sign into that account and watch the money add up. You'll learn what we know: Saving money can be fun!

HOW TO BUDGET

Although you can absolutely have a daily budget or a weekly budget that you stick to, most budgeting systems are monthly and based on how much you spend and earn over the course of a month. That's because most bills come in once a month. Once you've been budgeting a while, it's pretty incredible to look back over several months (or even several years!) and see patterns of your spending and saving start to take shape. In many ways, your budget is like a living diary of all the things you do and the adventures you have. And many budgets can be written just as you would a journal: with bullets, colorful illustrations, and mementos of fun experiences you've had.

The beauty of your budget is that it's *yours*—and if you put a little time into it, it will be just as vibrant and successful as you are.

OUR FAVORITE BUDGET

There are lots of ways to budget, but we've found the best way is backwards. You set your big goals—putting savings first—and make everything else work around them. Here's an example.

Let's say you earn $2,000 each month after taxes are deducted from your paycheck. This is called your net income.

Your Backwards Budget looks like this:

$2,000 monthly net income

First, I will put:

$200 into my savings account

$100 into my investment account/stock portfolio (as we'll talk about later, your investments are a part of your savings—so when you add the first two items you get to the important 15%)

$100 toward my new car fund (goal = buy in two years)

After that, I spend on my needs:

$600 for rent

$200 on groceries

$100 on utilities

$300 for car payment and car insurance

$50 for health insurance

$80 for cell phone bill

$20 for charity

Once that's covered, I have:

$250 left for fun, entertainment, and other wants

So, essentially, a Backwards Budget has three steps:

1. Save for your goals first.
2. Pay for your needs.
3. Enjoy anything in the wants category with whatever you have left over.

THE 15/50/30 BREAKDOWN

If you're not sure exactly how to fill in the blanks to make the numbers work, tracking your spending for a month before you start can give you the information you need. But there are also some guidelines that can help:

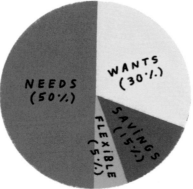

Those of you doing the math in your head know that those three numbers add up to 95% . . . so what about the other 5%? That's your wiggle room. If you're trying to save for something special, put it there. If you have an unexpected expense, it goes there. It's flexible.

HOW TO STAY ON TRACK

How you keep track of your budget is up to you—you can use an old-fashioned pen and paper, a digital spreadsheet, a bullet journal, or an app. There are LOTS of budgeting apps; some are free and some are not. Check out Mint (free) and YNAB (not) as you get going.

WHAT HAPPENS WHEN YOU GET OFF COURSE—AND HOW TO GET BACK ON TRACK

Guess what? We all make mistakes, so don't beat yourself up if you overspend one month. If you do get off track, take a step back and ask yourself what happened so you can get to the root of it. For example, if you went over budget because your favorite boots finally fell apart or your laptop died unexpectedly, it's okay to replace those items. But if you couldn't resist another pair of your favorite jeans, that's something to think twice about next time.

Here are a couple of tricks to keep you on target:

Set Up Mental Barriers to Overspending. Every time you reach for an impulse buy or you're tempted to click on that ad for something adorable, stop and think: *Do I need this?* Take twenty-four hours and think about whether you really want something or not. You may be surprised that you forget all about that item that you just "had to have" a few short days ago.

Reward Yourself. When you reach your goals in life, that's cause for celebration, and your financial goals are no different. Reward yourself when you hit certain milestones by buying an item or experience you've been wanting. It's important for your brain to know that sticking with a budget = good things.

TL;DR

CHAPTER 5 KEY TAKEAWAYS

- Budgeting is one of the main building blocks to financial success. It's actively planning your spending so you know where your money is going to go.
- There are many ways to budget, but our favorite is the Backwards Budget. You can choose the budget that works best for you. There are also many apps you can use to stay on track.
- We're all going to go over budget, make mistakes, and overspend occasionally. It happens. Set up mental barriers to overspending by taking time to decide: *Do I really need or want this item?*

ATHENA VALENTINE

FOUNDER AND CEO OF MONEY SMART LATINA

WHICH WORDS DEFINE YOU?

Dynamic, independent, self-starter, outgoing, empathetic, resourceful.

WHAT'S YOUR JOB?

I'm a student development manager for Jobs for Arizona's Graduates, a nonprofit. I help first-generation high school students remove barriers to their success while transitioning onto a postsecondary of their choice. I also run the website Money Smart Latina!

WHAT'S THE CHANGE YOU'RE LOOKING TO CREATE IN THE WORLD?

I was homeless in high school after my mom died my freshman year, which led me to become scrappy like Alexander Hamilton. I want everyone to know that your demographics do not determine your destiny.

TELL US ABOUT YOUR FIRST JOB.

My first job was as a floater for a Boys and Girls Club. If someone called in sick or had a vacation, I took over their area. My starting salary was $5.15 an hour. I can't even buy a mocha for that now!

WHAT'S THE BIGGEST MONEY MISTAKE YOU EVER MADE?

Cashing in my 403(b) [retirement account] during a bad breakup. At the time, I had undiagnosed mental health issues, which caused me to swipe my card a lot. I'm definitely not proud of it, but since then, I've learned healthy coping mechanisms, and I no longer make it rain at Sephora.

WHAT'S THE SMARTEST MONEY MOVE YOU EVER MADE?

The smartest money move I've ever made was starting my own business. I'm a firm believer in having more than one income stream.

TELL US A MONEY STORY THAT MADE YOU WHO YOU ARE TODAY.

After my mom passed away, I was bitter and angry, but now, I use my experience to help others who may be in the same situation and need an advocate.

WHAT ONE PIECE OF CAREER ADVICE WOULD YOU GIVE TO YOUR YOUNGER SELF?

ALWAYS NEGOTIATE YOUR INCOME! I was an underearner for YEARS, and it wasn't until after I realized I couldn't save what I didn't make, I started to negotiate my pay and find various ways to bring extra income in.

WHAT ONE PIECE OF MONEY ADVICE WOULD YOU GIVE TO YOUR YOUNGER SELF?

Don't cash in your retirement account to go shopping.

WHAT ARE THE THREE MOST IMPORTANT THINGS YOU WISH EVERYONE KNEW ABOUT BUDGETING?

1. Try to save on living expenses. This will be the biggest line item in your budget, so make sure you do research before moving out. Save way more than you think you need because if no one else tells you, FURNITURE IS SO EXPENSIVE.

2. You do have food at home. Eating out can easily add up to hundreds of dollars a month, so try to set a weekly limit and then cut yourself off.

3. If you are going to get a pet, get pet insurance. The love of my life has so many health issues, he's cost me over $10,000.

6

HEY, WHERE'S MY MONEY?

Banks, Checking and Savings Accounts, Debit Cards, and More

Did you have a piggy bank growing up? Maybe you still have one—with coins rattling around inside every time you pick it up. That's great for storing your spare change (you'll be surprised at how quickly it adds up), but before you get out of high school or as soon as you start working, you're going to want an account at a bank or credit union.

FYI, this wasn't always possible for women. Until the 1960s when women started entering the workforce in large numbers, women couldn't open our own bank accounts. Even then, in many cases, we had to have the permission of husbands or other male relatives. And it wasn't until the Equal Credit Opportunity Act of 1974—fifty-four years after women got the right to vote—that it became illegal to deny giving someone a bank account or a credit card based on their sex, race, or marital status. With this act, women could finally begin saving in their own accounts in banks or credit unions and getting credit cards in their own names.

EQUAL CREDIT OPPORTUNITY ACT

1974

1950   1960   1970   1980

BANKS VS. CREDIT UNIONS: WHAT'S THE DIFFERENCE?

Banks are for-profit companies where you can keep money, save money, or borrow money. A for-profit company is a corporation or business of any kind that seeks to make a profit for its owners.

Credit unions are just like banks except they are not-for-profit organizations, owned and controlled by its members, which is what customers are called. (At a not-for-profit, also called a nonprofit organization, any money made goes toward funding bigger organizational goals. Charities are nonprofit organizations, too.)

Today, you have another choice as well—an online bank. Online banks differ from traditional banks in that they don't have physical locations that you can walk into. All business is conducted via the internet and apps. But besides that basic difference, they're still in the same business.

At both kinds of banks as well as at credit unions, you can do much of the same things: deposit your money into a menu of accounts (including checking and savings accounts) and borrow money by taking out a loan. Opening an account helps you to establish yourself financially by giving you a safe place to keep your money until you're ready to use it.

LOAN: Money that you borrow.

AND, YES, YOUR MONEY IS SAFE

You may have heard jokes about people who keep their money under the mattress due to fear. Some of those fears come from the Great

Depression. When the stock market crashed in 1929, thousands of banks closed without warning, and people lost their life savings. Thankfully, we don't have to worry about that anymore.

The Banking Act of 1933 created the Federal Deposit Insurance Corporation (FDIC), which insures the nation's banking system against collapse. When you see "FDIC Insured," that's a sign you can trust your bank or credit union to keep your money—up to $250,000 per depositor—secure.

PROS AND CONS: BANKS VS. CREDIT UNIONS VS. ONLINE BANKS

So how do you decide where to open your first account? Let's use one of our favorite tools, the pro/con list!

BANKS

PROS	CONS
✓ MORE LOCATIONS	✗ REQUIRE A MINIMUM BALANCE TO OPEN AN ACCOUNT
✓ BETTER APPS/ TECHNOLOGY	✗ STRICTER RULES AND LESS FLEXIBILITY
✓ ANYONE CAN JOIN	✗ HIGHER FEES

CREDIT UNION

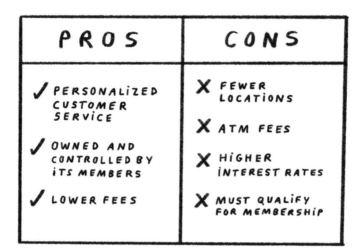

PROS	CONS
✔ PERSONALIZED CUSTOMER SERVICE	✘ FEWER LOCATIONS
✔ OWNED AND CONTROLLED BY ITS MEMBERS	✘ ATM FEES
✔ LOWER FEES	✘ HIGHER INTEREST RATES
	✘ MUST QUALIFY FOR MEMBERSHIP

ONLINE BANKS

PROS	CONS
✔ BETTER INTEREST AND LOAN RATES	✘ SOME DON'T OFFER ATM CARDS
✔ LOW OR NO MINIMUM BALANCE REQUIREMENTS AND NO FEES	✘ NO BRANCHES TO WALK INTO
✔ overall GENERALLY GOOD TECHNOLOGY	✘ NO PHYSICAL PLACE TO DEPOSIT CHECKS

The Verdict: Many people decide not to choose. They keep their checking accounts at a traditional bank or credit union nearby and their savings accounts in an online bank to earn more interest. Then they transfer money back and forth between the accounts online (it's easy). There are no rules restricting you on which accounts you can have in which banks or how many you can have. (Though there are often rules on the number of transfers you can make from your savings, so read the fine print first!) Just make sure you compare perks, fees, convenience, and interest rates before you sign on the dotted line.

OPENING YOUR FIRST ACCOUNT

The differences between traditional banks, online banks, and credit unions give you the big picture. To help you pick one individual bank or credit union, ask your family and friends what they use. Convenience matters. If you're not driving yet, using your parents' bank is probably going to be the way to go. But you can also go online or call to find out: Is there a monthly account fee and how much is it? Is there a minimum you have to deposit to get started? Are there ATM fees, and if so, how much?

You can set up an account online or in person. In order to fill out the application—which will ask for your birth date, Social Security Number, address, and phone number—you'll need:

- **ID:** Most banks require two forms of identification such as a driver's license, passport, or birth certificate.
- **A parent or guardian if you're under eighteen:** If you're not yet of age, you'll need an adult co-owner to join the account with you and fill out forms on your behalf.
- **An initial deposit to put into the account.** For some banks, this can be as little as $20, but others require $100, $500, or more.

Once your application is in, the bank or credit union will run a quick online check of your past banking history. As soon as it's done, your account will be approved and ready to go, and you'll get your ATM card, checks, and any other items you requested in the mail.

CHECKING ACCOUNTS

There are two basic types of accounts at banks and credit unions: checking accounts and savings accounts. You're going to want both. Keep in mind that you must be at least fourteen years old to open a bank account, and no one under the age of eighteen can open an account in their name alone. Once you turn fourteen, you and your legal guardian can open an account together, and once you turn eighteen, you can own the account yourself, no co-owner required.

A checking account is a day-to-day transaction or spending account. When you get paid, your money will usually go into your checking account—sometimes by direct deposit, which means it goes there automatically from your employer. Then you'll spend the money from your checking account. You will also get an ATM/debit card on this account that you can use to make purchases or pull cash out of the ATM (Automatic Teller Machine) when you need it. You can link the account to payment apps like Venmo and Zelle and use it to move money between friends. (More on these in a moment.)

You'll also use this account to pay your bills (once you have some). In most cases, this happens online. You'll receive bills by email or regular mail, then sign onto your bank's online portal or app and pay them. (Sometimes you'll pay them on the biller's website instead.)

Occasionally, though, you may need to write a paper check. Over the last few decades, checks have become a rarer method of payment. Digital payments are not just faster, they're greener—no paper!—and they're easier, but you still need to know how to write a check.

SAVINGS ACCOUNTS: EARNING MONEY ON YOUR MONEY

A **savings account** is a bank account where you put money that you don't want to spend but rather, well, save! Savings accounts pay you for keeping your money in the bank—essentially giving the bank permission to borrow your money to do various bank things. (Don't worry, it's still yours!) This payment is called **interest**.

Interest is a big topic that we'll dive into in more detail in just a moment. But you should know up front that it applies to both money you earn (like interest added to your savings account) and money you owe (like interest added to a loan you have to repay). First off, interest is calculated in percentages and relates back to something called your principal. This is the amount of your original loan or deposit into your savings account. Simple interest is calculated by multiplying the interest rate by the principal over a period of time.

For example, let's say on January 1, you were to deposit $1,000

INTEREST = PRINCIPAL X RATE X TIME

into a savings account. And that savings account has a simple annual interest rate (or annual percentage rate, APR) of 5%. This means you'd earn 5% on that $1,000 by the end of the year—at which point you'd have $1,050.

But if you've ever seen an ad from a bank, you know most banks compound interest not annually but daily. This is a good thing for you. What it means is that instead of paying you the whole 5% at the end of the year, they divide it up into 365 itsy-bitsy interest payments and then—and this is the compounding part—every day, they add the prior day's interest to your new principal and pay you interest on the new total. Essentially, you earn interest on your interest. And that's how your money grows!

GROWTH OF SAVINGS ACCOUNT

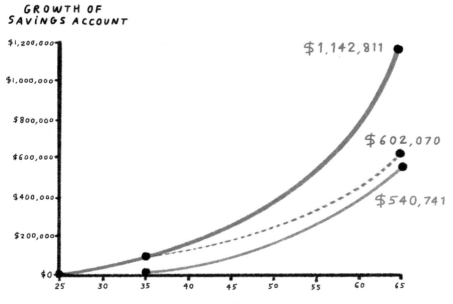

$1,142,811

$602,070

$540,741

AGE

Let's say instead that on January 1, you were to deposit $1,000 at an APR of 5% *compounded daily*, then at the end of the year, you'd have $1,052—that's $2 more!

Who cares about $2? Well, you should. Because as you'll see when we talk about the interest you pay on credit cards (in chapter 7) or earn on your investments (in chapter 8), compound interest can be your worst enemy or your very best friend.

P.S., You know that 5% interest rate we used in the example? Unfortunately, you're not going to find that anywhere. When we wrote this book in 2021, bank savings accounts were paying less than 1%—even the best ones, called high-yield savings accounts, were paying less than 1%. In 2021 (as we're writing this book), the Federal Funds rate—a short-term interest rate set by the government, on which bank savings rates are based—is very low. Over time, it will go up and down, but it always pays to shop around for the best savings rates you can find. Just Google "best high-yield savings accounts." Voilà.

SAVINGS ACCOUNT PERMA-STASH: YOUR EMERGENCY FUND

Emergencies happen. Cars break down. Phones get wet and die. A pet needs medical care. You need money to deal with all of those things—in advance—and a specific savings account called an Emergency Fund is the best place for it. Here's a breakdown:

- **What Is an Emergency Fund?** It's your financial airbag. It provides a soft landing when you need money ASAP in order to fix a problem.
- **How Much Should I Have in an Emergency Fund?** Pick a number—$50, $100, or even $1,000 or more—that makes you feel good about being ready for a financial surprise. As you get older and have more responsibilities, the size of your emergency stash should grow. We recommend adults have enough to cover three to six months of living expenses.
- **Where Should I Keep It?** In the bank but in savings not checking. You'll be less tempted to spend it that way. Banks will happily help you open multiple savings accounts at no charge, so if you want one just for emergencies, feel free.
- **What *Is* an Emergency, Exactly?** It's something you truly need—not your "I forgot it was my friend's birthday, and I don't have enough money in my checking account to get her a gift" fund.

TWO MORE WAYS TO SAVE

When you're first starting your financial journey, checking and savings accounts are the way to go. But there are two other kinds of bank accounts to know about as well. Both are for money you don't need access to every day.

Money Market Accounts: These are savings accounts with some checking features. They generally give you a debit card and let you make a few withdrawals each month. They often have higher minimum balance requirements (meaning you need more money just to open one) than regular savings, but they also tend to pay a little more interest.

CDs (Certificates of Deposit): Not compact discs. In a financial context, a CD is a certificate of deposit, a type of savings account where you deposit your money for a certain amount of time without taking it out. CDs typically range from three months to five years, and the longer you agree to let the bank keep the money, the more interest you typically earn. The catch is you can't take it out until the CD term is up or until it has "matured." What if you need the money? You can get it, but you'll usually pay a penalty for "breaking" the CD.

DEPOSITS AND WITHDRAWALS

Putting money into your accounts is called making a deposit. Pulling it out is called making a withdrawal.

In years past, people did this in person at the bank. They'd fill out a deposit slip or withdrawal slip (which was kind of like writing a check), hand it over to the person behind the counter (called the teller), and—if you were like us at HerMoney—grab a DumDum lolly on the way out. (We always went for the butterscotch.)

You can still do that, but you no longer have to because . . . technology. You can use your own bank's ATMs to deposit checks and get cash. (You can use other banks' ATMs to get cash, too, but you shouldn't because you'll pay a fee of $2 to $3.50 on average each time.) You can also deposit checks using many bank and credit union apps by just endorsing it—signing your name—on the back, snapping a picture, and pressing deposit. Presto. Done.

And then there's direct deposit. Once you're earning a regular paycheck, direct deposit allows your employer to send money straight to your bank account. You don't have to get a paper check from your employer and manually deposit it. If your employer offers direct deposit, you'll be informed of it when you start your job and fill out your hiring paperwork. It's easy. You'll just provide your employer with your bank account number and routing number, and they'll make your deposits happen—directly!

However, if you ever have to go old-school, here are some handy guides to those bank slips:

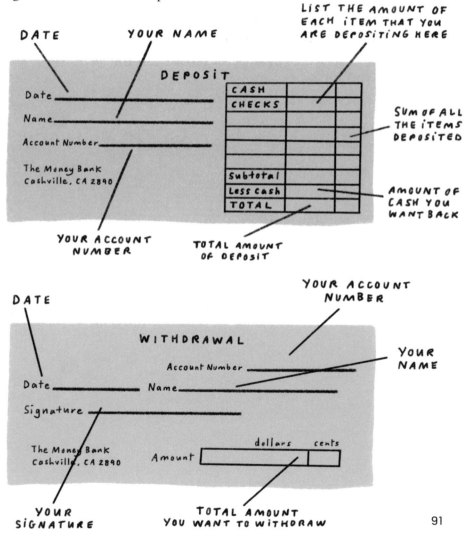

THE WONDERFUL WORLD OF DEBIT/ATM CARDS

When you open a checking account, you'll get a **debit card**. You can use this card to make purchases pretty much everywhere—and you can also use it to pull cash out of ATMs. A debit card is linked to your checking account. This means when you make a purchase, the money comes out immediately. It's kind of like spending cash without the hassle of having to go get cash to spend.

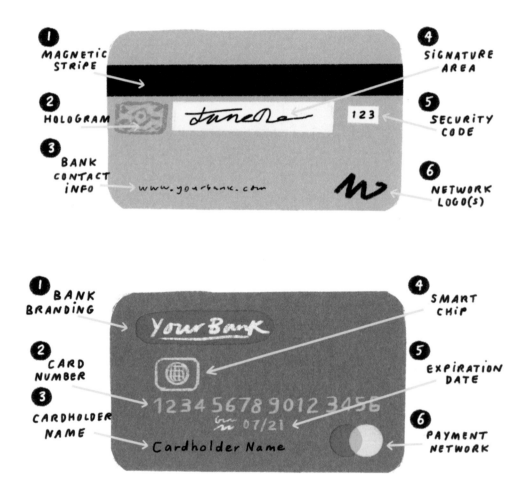

1 MAGNETIC STRIPE

2 HOLOGRAM

3 BANK CONTACT INFO

4 SIGNATURE AREA

5 SECURITY CODE

6 NETWORK LOGO(S)

1 BANK BRANDING

2 CARD NUMBER

3 CARDHOLDER NAME

4 SMART CHIP

5 EXPIRATION DATE

6 PAYMENT NETWORK

Two important things to know about your debit card. First, when you get one, you'll be asked if you want overdraft protection. Say no. If you opt in for this feature and you use your card without having enough money to pay for whatever you're buying, the bank will cover the cost then charge you an overdraft fee of about $35 (maybe more) for the privilege. (The same thing will happen if you spend more money than you have in the account in other ways, by paying bills automatically or by writing checks. This is called overdrawing.) You don't want or need this.

And second, losing your debit card or having it stolen—because it's linked to your checking account—is a big deal. If it falls into the wrong hands, your account could be wiped out. Yes, you'll likely get the money back, but it can take weeks, which is a huge pain. If you notice it missing, report it pronto. For the same reason, never share your PIN (Personal Identification Number), the passcode to your account.

TL;DR

CHAPTER 6 KEY TAKEAWAYS

- You need a place to keep your money safe. Banks (traditional or online) and credit unions are the ticket. Opening your first account is a great big step toward an adult financial life.
- When you open your first accounts, you'll probably stick with just a checking account (for money you spend on a week-to-week basis) and a savings account (for money you don't want to spend).
- A debit card will be likely be your primary bank tool. Use it wisely. And if you lose it, report it immediately.
- Your emergency fund belongs in a savings account—always.

POCKET
SUN

CO-FOUNDER OF SOGAL VENTURES, AN ORGANIZATION THAT CONNECTS ENTREPRENEURS WITH FUNDING

WHICH WORDS DEFINE YOU?

Visionary, inspiring, feminist, entrepreneur, investor.

WHAT'S YOUR JOB?

I'm on a mission to redefine the next generation of entrepreneurs and investors. I raised and currently manage a $15 million venture capital fund, SoGal Ventures, that invests in early stage, high-growth women and diverse entrepreneurs. I also run the SoGal Foundation.

WHAT'S THE CHANGE YOU'RE LOOKING TO CREATE IN THE WORLD?

I wish to enable more women to live on their own terms, to own at least 50% of the next big thing. I hope to invest in a future that is kind, empathetic, sustainable, and inclusive.

TELL US ABOUT YOUR FIRST JOB.

My first full-time job out of college was product marketing specialist at Motorola Solutions, making $55,000 a year. I worked with engineers to understand products they designed.

WHAT'S THE BIGGEST MONEY MISTAKE YOU EVER MADE?

I was scammed my freshman year in college when I first came to the US alone. I thought I could make some income by helping people wire money via Western Union, but the checks turned out to be fake. It was an expensive lesson.

WHAT'S THE SMARTEST MONEY MOVE YOU EVER MADE?

I invested in myself by taking a course about venture capital investing in Silicon Valley. I met my current business partner there, and we decided to start SoGal Ventures together. It changed my career forever.

WHAT'S THE MONEY SECRET YOU'RE KEEPING?

This is a secret that far too few women know. Investing in startups, aka angel investing, can fast track your career by five to ten years and can potentially generate life-changing money.

WHAT ONE PIECE OF CAREER ADVICE WOULD YOU GIVE TO YOUR YOUNGER SELF?

You have not even heard of the career you'll create for yourself. Don't get stuck in the competition in front of you right now; it'll fade away.

WHAT ONE PIECE OF MONEY ADVICE WOULD YOU GIVE TO YOUR YOUNGER SELF?

Start investing as early as possible because time is your friend. Start small and do it with a long-term mindset. Invest $1,000 in three to five of your favorite companies' stocks, and don't touch them until graduation.

WHAT ARE THE THREE BEST INVESTMENTS THAT PEOPLE CAN MAKE IN THEIR LIFETIME?

1. Invest in your own education and see more of the world.

2. Invest in startups (preferably founded by women).

3. Invest in the smartest people you meet, and keep meeting more smart people.

7

GIVE ME SOME CREDIT

Why Credit Is So Important to Your Bright Financial Future

You've probably heard the word *credit* used in lots of different contexts over the years. Perhaps you've seen people in movies or TV commercials complain that they have bad credit or celebrate that they just raised their credit score and were able to qualify for a home loan.

But what is it, really? Credit is basically the ability to borrow money from someone or something with the promise that you'll pay it back later.

In a lot of ways, though, it's like your GPA. If your GPA is higher, you have the ability to get into a better college and maybe get a scholarship. You may also have more opportunities to join honors societies or clubs as a result of your good grades.

The same is true of your credit. If it's good, it can open an awful lot of doors like the ability to buy a home, afford a car, or get a loan at a good price. But if your credit is bad—or if you just haven't built enough of it yet—it can make life harder and make borrowing more expensive.

LONGTIME CARDHOLDER

ALWAYS PAYS BILLS ON TIME

< 30%

USES LESS THAN 30% OF MAX. ALLOWANCE

GOOD CREDIT:

• Pay bills on time, every time.

• Use no more than 30% (and preferably less) of the maximum you're allowed on your credit cards.

• Maintain long credit relationships (10+ years is good).

• Don't apply for credit too often. If you have too many credit cards open in your name, lenders will start to see you as a higher risk.

• As you get older, try to apply for a mix of types of credit like a car loan and mortgage (or home loan) in addition to a credit card.

BAD CREDIT:

• Pay bills late.

• Outspend limit on credit card.

• Use credit cards to pay other credit cards.

• Only pay minimum balance on credit card bill/carry a balance.

• Not using your credit.

OWNS TOO MANY CREDIT CARDS

PAYS BILLS LATE

OUTSPENDS CARD LIMITS

YOUR CREDIT SCORE

A credit score is a financial grade that tells companies lending you money (banks, credit card companies, student lenders, auto lenders, even cell phone companies) how likely you are to pay your bills. Other types of companies use credit as a measure of how responsible you are—landlords, for instance, when they're deciding whether to rent you an apartment or insurance companies when they're deciding how much to charge you to insure your car.

Your credit score will be a number somewhere between zero and 850—the higher the better. Almost no one has an 850, and the truth is that you don't need a score that high. Once you hit 740, your credit is "very good," and at 800, it's "excellent." At this level, you'll be able to borrow money at the cheapest rates because you've shown you're responsible with your finances. Below 670, you're fair and will pay more to borrow, and below 580 (with the exception of federal student loans), you'll have trouble borrowing at all.

So what are you being graded on? And by whom? Let's take that second question first. There are three major credit bureaus in the US: Equifax, Experian, and TransUnion. These credit bureaus all have the same job; they report your payment history to the lenders you do business with. That history lands on your credit report, and the information on that report gets translated into a credit score. Lenders pull, or look at, your credit report when they're deciding whether to lend you money and how much to charge you for it in interest.

BUILDING A CREDIT-WORTHY REP

The goal is to build a positive credit reputation with every payment you make. Think of it this way: When you borrowed the family car from your parents for the very first time, they were probably nervous about it. They laid down rules, set expectations, determined consequences, and overall were pretty tough. However, after you borrowed the car a few times and made it home by curfew, they got more comfortable and allowed you to stay out later or roam farther from home. This was because you earned their trust. But if things hadn't gone well, the story would've been different. The rules would've gotten stricter, and they might not have let you borrow the car at all.

It's exactly the same thing when banks or credit card companies are lending you money for the first time. Because you have no credit history, the bank has no clue if they'll get paid back on time. This is why your first credit card will have a low limit, and if you take out a loan (with the exception of federal student loans), you'll pay a higher-than-average interest rate. But over time, if you prove you're a good person to lend to, you'll get offered better interest rates, higher credit limits, and better deals overall.

And credit is a marathon, not a sprint. Building it takes time. And even though you can make mistakes quickly, coming back from them takes time. Typically, mistakes like late payments stay on your credit report for seven years. But because your credit report is a living, breathing document—with new information being added every month—they hurt your score less and less as time goes by. After about two years, most mistakes don't matter much at all.

LET'S TALK ABOUT CREDIT CARDS

Credit cards, like debit cards, are used to buy things (you knew that, right?) to make purchases online or in a store. They look almost identical. They both feature your name on the front, along with a 16-digit card number, an expiration date, an additional identification code, and a chip. But behind the scenes, they work totally differently.

As we talked about last chapter, when you use a debit card, you're spending your own money. When you use a credit card, you're not. You're borrowing from the issuer of the card, usually a bank.

When you apply for—and get—your first credit card, you'll sign a user agreement that serves as your promise to pay back the credit card company. This user agreement also details how much you'll pay in interest if you can't pay your purchases off at the end of the grace period

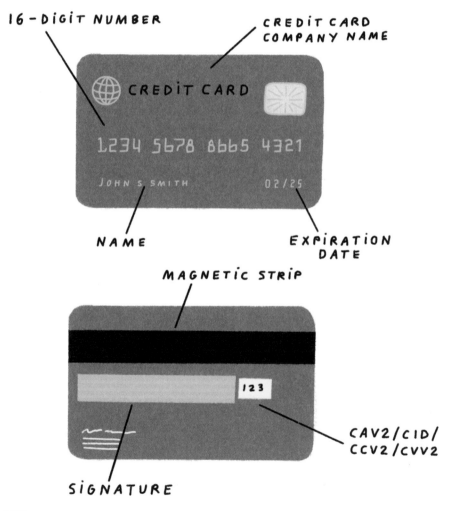

16-DIGIT NUMBER

CREDIT CARD COMPANY NAME

CREDIT CARD

1234 5678 8665 4321

JOHN S SMITH   02/25

NAME

EXPIRATION DATE

MAGNETIC STRIP

123

CAV2/CID/ CCV2/CVV2

SIGNATURE

you get following the month or billing cycle in which you buy them. Grace periods are usually between 21 and 25 days. It also tells you the credit limit, which is the maximum amount you're allowed to charge on your card.

Credit card interest rates—unlike the small amount you earn by putting your money in the bank—can add up *fast*. As we write this, credit card interest rates average about 15% but can go much higher, particularly for people who don't have a long credit history (like you).

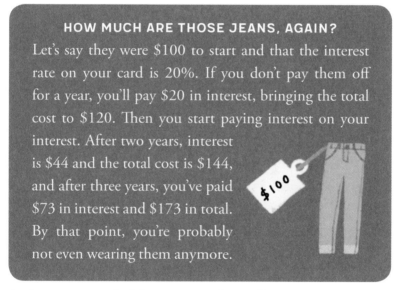

HOW MUCH ARE THOSE JEANS, AGAIN?

Let's say they were $100 to start and that the interest rate on your card is 20%. If you don't pay them off for a year, you'll pay $20 in interest, bringing the total cost to $120. Then you start paying interest on your interest. After two years, interest is $44 and the total cost is $144, and after three years, you've paid $73 in interest and $173 in total. By that point, you're probably not even wearing them anymore.

And once you rack debt up, it can be really hard to get out of. This gets tough because credit card companies don't make you pay off their bills in full every month. All they require is a minimum payment that's usually around 3% of your bill. But don't fall for the minimum payment trap! It's a way to find yourself in debt for years because the credit card company charges you interest on the amount left over when you only pay the minimum. Each time that remaining balance grows and you get hit with that added interest, the amount you owe gets bigger and bigger.

If you have credit card debt of $1,000
And your credit card charges interest of 15%
And you only pay the minimum every month,
It will take you 106 months—or nearly nine years—to pay off.
Over that time, you'll pay an additional $729.18 in interest.
Holy crap.

All of which is to say, when you do get a credit card, use it wisely. In most cases, only charge things you can pay off the month you buy them. If and when you break that rule, make sure you have a concrete plan for paying off the purchases before too much time has passed.

iF THEY'RE SO DANGEROUS, WHY SHOULD YOU GET ONE?

Four reasons: 1) If you're smart (which you are) and play by the paying-things-off-as-you-buy-them rules we've laid out here, they're not dangerous. 2) They're really useful in an emergency. 3) They are very handy in helping you build credit. 4) You'll eventually be able to earn rewards like points for travel.

In other words, getting a credit card is probably something you'll want to do. So when is the right time? And what kind of card should you get?

YOUR FIRST CREDIT CARD

There are three ways a credit card will make its way into your wallet.

First, you could apply for a student card and get it. Anyone who is eighteen or older can apply for a credit card. You won't be approved for one unless you can show some kind of steady income on the application. If you have a job with steady income, look online for good starter credit cards by Googling "first credit cards" or "student credit cards." These starter cards tend to have low credit limits—which means they will only allow you to spend a certain (lower) amount of money before they cut you off. They also tend to have higher-than-average interest rates.

Second, if you don't qualify for a card based on your income or credit history, you can apply for a secured credit card. These act (and look) just like regular credit cards except you have to give the issuer some money—called a deposit—down just in case you don't pay your bills. This is called collateral. The amount you deposit, usually a few hundred dollars, becomes your credit limit. You then have the ability to spend that amount on your card and get started on your credit-building journey. They're not perfect because the interest rates tend to be high. But if you pay them off regularly and use them wisely, eventually you'll get your deposit back and start to build credit in the process. They can be a perfect entry point into the world of credit.

The third option is to ask your parents if they can make you an authorized user on one of their cards, which you can do even if you're under eighteen. Your parents call their credit card company and request a credit card for you in your name but on their account. They can even set a separate credit limit for your card. The upside is you'll start building a credit history since the credit card companies will start reporting the payment history under your name. The downside? Your parent's credit history gets added to your credit report, too. If their credit is good, that's a bonus. But if it's not so good? Steer clear of this move. There's also a risk to your parents if you aren't responsible with the card because—even if you agree to pay your parents in real time for all the money you spend—authorized users are not legally liable for paying off the balances they run up. Make sure everyone understands what's going on before you proceed here.

CREDIT CARDS VS. DEBIT CARDS: WHICH TO USE WHEN

YOU'RE TRYING TO STAY ON BUDGET: DEBIT (Because when you're spending your own money, the temptation to spend isn't as great.)

YOU'RE TRYING TO BUILD CREDIT: CREDIT (Your behavior with debit cards isn't reported to the credit bureaus.)

YOU DON'T HAVE THE MONEY TO PAY FOR IT THIS MONTH: Ummmm. Think again. Credit is the only way to get it now. (But maybe the better plan is to wait to buy it when you can afford to pay for it?)

YOU'RE SHOPPING ONLINE FROM AN UNKNOWN SITE: CREDIT (Your credit card company will have your back if it turns out to be a scam.)

YOU WANT TO EARN REWARDS: CREDIT (Credit cards pay more rewards than debit cards do.)

WHAT A GOOD FIRST CREDIT CARD LOOKS LIKE

Never forget that credit card companies are running a business—the more cards you open, and the more you pay in interest and fees, the more money they make! They will always be enticing new customers with "unbeatable" offers, but you should never apply for anything until you've done your research. Rarely are the credit card offers you get in the mail the best ones available.

ONCE YOU HAVE INCOME TO SUPPORT A CARD OF YOUR OWN, A GOOD FIRST CREDIT CARD WILL HAVE:

Checklist

NO ANNUAL FEE ☑

AN AVERAGE OR BELOW INTEREST RATE ☑

LOW FEES ☑

CASH BACK ☑

No Annual Fee. Some credit cards have annual fees of anywhere from $20 to $500 per year. But other cards are completely free. Usually, the more rewards a card has, the more it charges, and eventually they may be worth paying for but probably not yet. Just make sure you read the fine print. Some cards waive the annual fee for the first year but then start charging you. You want free forever.

A Reasonable Interest Rate. Granted, you may be thinking, *What does the interest rate matter if I'm going to pay off my card every month?* And yes, sometimes you have to pay a higher interest rate on your first card. But expenses happen, and there's no point locking yourself into a super-high interest rate if there's a cheaper one available.

Low Fees. Take a look at how much you'll be charged if you accidentally pay late one month. Also look at how much foreign transaction fees cost if you use your card in another country. (Sometimes it's nothing, sometimes it's as much as 3% of the purchase.)

Cash Back. Many cards these days offer cash back for spending. Although it can be tough to find cards with no annual fees that give you primo credit card rewards, you can find ones that give you cash back. That's the best starter reward.

THE FiNE PRiNT

Every credit card comes with terms you agree to in order to hold a card, here's what they mean:

COST OF BORROWING FROM YOUR CREDIT CARD iSSUER

Rates and Fees Table

Interest Rates	
A Annual Percentage Rate (APR) for Purchases	**Prime Rate + 14.99%** This is a variable APR. See *Explanation of Variable Rates* below.

Penalty APR and When it Applies	**Prime Rate + 25.99%**
	
	 This is a variable APR. See *Explanation of Variable Rates* below.
	
	 This APR will apply to your account if you:
	    1) make one or more late payments; or
	    2) make a payment that is returned by your bank.
	
	 We may also consider your creditworthiness in determining whether or not to apply the penalty APR to your Account.
	
	 How Long Will the Penalty APR Apply? If the penalty APR is applied, it will apply for at least 6 months. We will review your Account every 6 months after the penalty APR is applied. The penalty APR will continue to apply until you have made timely payments with no returned payments during the 6 months being reviewed.

B Paying Interest	Your due date is at least 25 days after the close of each billing period. We will not charge you interest on purchases if you pay each month your entire balance (or, if you have a plan outstanding, your balance adjusted for plans) by the due date. We will begin charging interest on cash advances and balance transfers on the transaction date.
C For Credit Card Tips from the Consumer Financial Protection Bureau	**To learn more about factors to consider when applying for or using a credit card, visit the website of the Consumer Financial Protection Bureau at http://www.consumerfinance.gov/learnmore**
Fees	
D Annual Membership Fee	**$49**
Transaction Fees • Foreign Transaction	**2.7%** of each transaction after conversion to US dollars.

E   Penalty Fees
    • Late Payment
    • Returned Payment
    • Overlimit
	Up to **$40**
	 Up to **$40**
	 None

The language on credit card agreements is standard for all companies—we pulled this one from Amex, which is the country's largest credit card issuer.

A. APR: (Annual Percentage Rate): The cost of borrowing from your credit card issuer, in percentage terms, including your interest rate and any additional fees.

B. Paying Interest: This tells you how to avoid paying interest charges on what you charge to your credit card. Paying your bill on time every month, in full, is the only way to avoid paying interest.

C. Credit Card Tips: The Consumer Financial Protection Bureau (CFPB) helps educate people on how to avoid credit card debt, how to protect yourself from identity theft, and more. Many of us will have questions before applying for our first credit card, and the CFBP is a great place to start.

D. Membership Fee (aka "annual fee"): The amount you'll pay each year to your credit card company for using your card. Some credit cards have no annual fee, and for your first card, you should look for one that's free.

E. Penalty Fees: These are the fees you'll pay if you miss a monthly payment, or if you are late on a payment.

WHAT ELSE DO YOU NEED TO KNOW ABOUT REWARDS?

Maybe you've heard stories about people jetting off on trips to Paris or Hawaii, which was all paid for by their credit card points, and you wished you could do the same. Eventually, you will be able to. But it's also easy to spend more trying to earn rewards than they're worth. The bottom line is that rewards and points are never worth going into debt. Yet 40% of people who have a rewards credit card carry a balance on their cards. The math there just doesn't work out.

Eventually, you may be spending enough on your credit cards to focus on earning other rewards. Just know that the best way to play this game is to a) choose your rewards card carefully, b) put as many of your everyday expenses on that card as you can, and c) pay that card off each month. That's how you get to Paris for a song.

PROTECT YOUR CREDIT AND YOUR IDENTITY
As you start to build your financial life, not only do you need to watch out for your own mistakes, but also, unfortunately, you've got to worry about bad guys, too. Identity theft is frighteningly common—over 14

million people per year have their identities stolen and millions of them are kids.

What is identity theft? It's when someone takes your personal information—your Social Security Number, birth date, address, or other details—and uses that info to open new credit card accounts, get a tax refund, or make any other financial moves in your name. For that reason, identity thieves are also always looking for little nuggets of personal information that they can use to pretend to be you in order to get access to this information. So how do you protect yourself?

Use Complex Passwords
If your dog's name is your password for every app and website that you use and just one of your accounts gets compromised, this means all of your accounts would be at risk. Whenever you're creating online accounts, be sure to use complex passwords and use a different password for each account. It can be hard to remember a hundred different passwords—this is where using your browser's password manager can help.

Don't Share Your Social Security Number
Your SSN is like the key to the kingdom, so keep it as private as possible. Some companies and services will ask you for your Social Security Number as a reliable way to tie your data together with other sources . . . But you can say no. Legally, you're not required to give your SSN to anyone other than the federal government.

Read the Fine Print

When visiting websites or signing up for online services, it's so easy to click "accept" without actually knowing what you're agreeing to. Take the time to read—or at least skim—the privacy policies of the websites and apps that you use so you'll know how your personal data will be protected.

Be Careful What You Share on Social Media

Let's go back to that example of using your dog's name as your password. What would it take to hack into your account if someone saw her cute puppy face all over your Instagram (with her dog tag and name in full view) . . .

Or let's say your password is your birth date. It wouldn't take much to guess your login if someone saw the roughly one thousand pictures your friends tagged you in at your party last year . . .

♥ 95 likes

♥ 32 likes

In other words, a scroll through your news feed is all someone needs to guess your password, which is just one of the reasons why you should limit how much personal information you share on social media. Even sharing any details about the city you live in could be enough to put you at risk.

Plus what you share on social media could even cost you a job. A survey by CareerBuilder found some 70% of companies check social media when screening job candidates, and of those, 57% discovered posts, images, or videos of some kind that made them decide not to hire someone.

FREEZE YOUR CREDIT

Unless you're actively shopping for a loan or credit card, freezing your credit prevents anyone from getting access to your credit report (even you), which means that no lender will be able to grant you credit. When you're still in your teens—and not ready for a credit card— freezing your credit is a very good protective move. It prevents identity thieves from messing with your credit before you even get started. Ask your parents to help you freeze it by going to the three credit bureaus: Experian.com, Equifax.com, and TransUnion.com. (They should probably freeze their own as well.) When you're ready to apply for your first card, you'll need to lift the freeze by revisiting those same credit bureaus. But it's easy—fifteen minutes and you'll be done with all three.

HOW TO KNOW if YOU'RE A VICTIM

You shouldn't have a credit report until you start building credit. But if one exists under your name and Social Security Number before that, it could be a sign that something's fishy. Ask your parents to pull your credit reports (one from each bureau) for free at AnnualCreditReport.com.

If there's information on it that doesn't belong to you, head to IdentityTheft.gov, the federal government's resource site, for step-by-step advice on what to do.

TL;DR

CHAPTER 7 KEY TAKEAWAYS

- Credit. Credit score. Bad credit. Good credit. Your credit is a measure of how responsible you are in America today. With good credit, landlords will want to rent to you. Insurers will give you better prices. Good credit also allows you to borrow money for things like homes and cars at lower prices.
- Credit cards are a great way to build credit, but they can do enormous, lasting damage to your financial future—and cost you a lot in interest—if you don't pay them off in a timely way.
- Credit cards and debit cards may look alike, but they work totally differently. When you use credit, you're borrowing money. When you use debit, you're spending your own.
- The number one rule for anyone with a credit card is to pay your balance in full every month. If you can't, make sure you have a plan for paying off what you owe in a reasonable amount of time.
- Identity theft—where someone uses your personal information to apply for credit in your name—is a big problem. You can stay safe by protecting your personal information on social media, using complex passwords, and freezing your credit.

TiFFANY ALiCHE

FOUNDER AND CEO OF THE BUDGETNISTA

WHICH WORDS DEFINE YOU?

Fierce, financial, funny, educator, compassionate.

WHAT'S YOUR JOB?

I am a financial educator. I help women achieve their financial goals through knowledge, access, and community.

WHAT'S THE CHANGE YOU'RE LOOKING TO CREATE IN THE WORLD?

I want women to feel confident about making financial decisions for themselves and their families. I want all women to have access to the tools, resources, and support they need in order to achieve their financial goals.

TELL US ABOUT YOUR FIRST JOB.

At age twenty-two, I was hired for my first real job. I was a preschool teacher in Newark, New Jersey, making $39,000/year. I managed to save over $40,000 in almost three years.

WHAT'S THE BIGGEST MONEY MISTAKE YOU EVER MADE?

At twenty-four, based upon the advice of a "friend," I took out a $20,000 cash advance and quite literally handed the cash over to A THIEF. I'd been told I'd make my money back within a few weeks, and I was blinded by the fact that I wanted to help my parents financially. They had sacrificed so much by raising and putting my four sisters and me through college. But instead of finding success, in less than one week, I went from having no credit card debt to being $35,000 in the hole. Yikes!

WHAT'S THE SMARTEST MONEY MOVE YOU EVER MADE?

Once I paid off my debt, I used my excess cash to earn and grow wealth via my business, The Budgetnista. I eventually earned enough money to pay off my parent's house, to purchase my dream home, and to purchase a money-making investment property—all in cash.

WHAT'S THE MONEY SECRET YOU ARE KEEPING?

Up until two years ago, I was not investing for retirement. Most of my money sat in a savings account. Even though I knew I was losing money by not investing, I was still afraid because of the investment mistake I made that left me $35,000 in debt. I broke free by hiring a financial planner, who helped guide me through my fear of investing.

WHAT ONE PIECE OF CAREER ADVICE WOULD YOU GIVE TO YOUR YOUNGER SELF?

All of your limitations are self-imposed. It's possible to do good work, help good people, and make good money. My life is proof.

WHAT ONE PIECE OF MONEY ADVICE WOULD YOU GIVE TO YOUR YOUNGER SELF?

Try to resist the FREE, FREE, FREE signs around campus advertising credit cards. You only need one, and you need to pay it off every month.

WHAT THREE THINGS DID YOU LEARN WHEN PAYING OFF YOUR CREDIT CARD DEBT?

1. Get-rich-quick schemes never (ever!) work.

2. Before making major decisions, ask for help from people you trust.

3. This too shall pass. Despite thinking things would never get better for me, they eventually did. Things do get better if you put the work in.

$$8$$

iNVESTiNG = MAKiNG MONEY iN YOUR SLEEP

When You're an Investor, Your Money Is Always Working for You.

In our working lives, we can only earn so much. Sure, we can take on a second job or get a side hustle, but there are only so many hours in the day. If only we could take the money we earn and grow it into more money without having to lift a finger . . . That's exactly what you can do by investing.

When you're investing, you're putting the dollars you've already saved into something that has the potential to grow over time. Think of investing like baking bread: You put your dough in the oven, expose it to heat, wait a while, and eventually it will rise. In other words, the oven does most of the work. While your bread is baking, you can sit back, relax, and focus on other things.

WHY WE iNVEST PART I: BECAUSE iNFLATiON SUCKS. LiTERALLY.

The goal of investing isn't simply about amassing a bigger pile of money for bragging rights (aka the travel photos we'll post on Insta, although those are very nice). There are some very practical reasons we all *need* our savings to grow over time—so we'll have more money later in life. The biggest reason is a pesky phenomenon called inflation.

You know that older relative who occasionally exclaims, "Back when I was your age, this [waves around random item] cost just [names some fraction of a dollar]!"? That's inflation at work. They don't say that because the item was actually cheaper then; they say that because the price has been inflated.

Inflation is like a slow leak to your spending power. As time goes on, the price of things like homes, cars, college, coffee, and flip-flops rise. Thankfully, so do salaries, but what *doesn't* go up is the value of your savings if you simply shove what you earn in a piggy bank or bank account paying nothing in interest. Fast forward twenty-five years and there you are, yelling at the robot cashier, "Back in my day, a burrito cost just $10! Now all that gets me is a plain tortilla!" To put it another way, inflation sucks the spending power from your savings.

The way to beat inflation (and make sure that $10 you put away twenty-five years ago grows enough so you can afford to buy a burrito, beverage, side of guacamole, chips, *and* queso) is to make your money grow faster than inflation. You do that by investing.

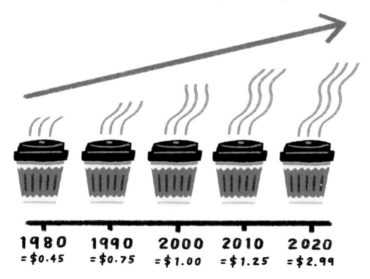

1980	1990	2000	2010	2020
= $0.45	= $0.75	= $1.00	= $1.25	= $2.99

WHY WE iNVEST PART II: BECAUSE COMPOUND iNTEREST

Compound interest is simply earning interest on your interest. It's *the most* important concept in all of money management. When we talked about it in chapter 6 in the context of savings accounts, the numbers weren't big because saving account interest rates are very low. In the world of investing, the numbers get bigger and more interesting. Let's see this thing in action:

Say you have $100 and invest it somewhere where it earns 10% per year. At the end of the first year, you'll have $110 in your account ($10 is 10% of $100). The following year you'll be paid 10% interest on $110. Interest continues to compound on ever-growing balances like that, year after year, until in twenty years you have $673 *without adding one additional dollar of your own money to your initial $100 investment.*

Thanks to compound interest, you earned $573 on your investment without lifting a finger.

How a single $100 investment grows over time earning a 10% average annual return

Year 1	Year 5	Year 10	Year 15	Year 20
$110	$161	$259	$418	$673

Now look at how much faster your money grows if you add $100 every year to your original $100 investment:

How investing $100 each year grows over time earning a 10% average annual return

Year 1	Year 5	Year 10	Year 15	Year 20
$210	$772	$1,853	$3,595	$6,400

That's the trick to supersizing your savings. You've invested $2,000 of your own money over twenty years and end up with $6,400.

It's likely that as the years go on, you'll be able to afford to save and invest much more than $100 a year. If you invest $500 each month while earning a 10% annual return, you'll have more than $360,000 twenty years from now—$240,000 from earning interest alone!

How investing $500 each month ($6,000 a year) grows over time while earning a 10% average annual return

Year 1	Year 5	Year 10	Year 15	Year 20
$6,835	$39,541	$103,776	$209,462	$383,348

YOUR SAVINGS SUPERPOWER: IT'S ABOUT TIME

Take a look at three investors.

Each saves $1,000 a month for ten years and earns a 7% return until age sixty-five. But they start the savings clock at different ages.

Kim saves from age twenty-five to age thirty-five.
Kate saves from age thirty-five to forty-five.
Kali saves from age forty-five to fifty-five.

Remember, they all invested the same amount ($120,000) over a decade and then let their money ride, continuing to earn interest. Here's how much each would have when they turn sixty-five:

Kim: $1.4 million
Kate: $734,000
Kali: $373,000

Simply by starting to save at a younger age, Kim ends up with twice as much money as Kate and four times as much as Kali. Crazy but true.

THE RULE OF 72 (AKA A WAY TO IMPRESS YOUR FRIENDS WITH FAST MATH)

The rule of 72 is a simple compound interest calculation you can use to see how long it will take to double your money. The formula is: 72 divided by the annual interest rate you expect to earn. For example, if you earned 8% on your savings, your money would double in nine years (72/8 = 9). Practice your simple division, and when the mood strikes, toss out this little nugget whenever there's an awkward pause in conversation.

THE RISK YOU TAKE: IT CAN BE INTIMIDATING

The big difference between saving money in a bank and investing it by buying shares of publicly traded companies called stocks (or the other investments we'll talk about in a sec) can be described in one word: risk.

When you put money into a savings account, you're guaranteed to earn a certain rate of interest. It's not a lot, but it's guaranteed. Even though, historically, the stock market has earned money for investors over time, it *is* possible to lose money, which is why you have to be careful how much you invest and which stocks—or other investments—you put it in.

So how do you decide whether to save your money or invest it? That depends on what the money is for and when you'll need to use it. The longer between when you make your investment and when you need the money, the more risk you can take. In general, if you need the money within the next three years, it belongs in the bank. If you don't need it for three or more, you can start thinking about investing it.

How do you decide how much to invest in the market? The answer to that question depends on your appetite for risk. It's a funny term that you might be able to guess the meaning of even if you've never heard it before—it means the amount of risk you're "hungry" for or the amount of risk you're willing to take with your money. Some people may be so eager to make money in the stock market that they'll take on as much risk as they can in the hopes of earning more, which means they have a *high* risk appetite. Other people are more fearful of losing their investment, so they choose safer stock market options. These people have a *low* risk appetite.

In the coming pages, we'll talk about ways to ensure you're not risking too much of your money. The goal is to get to a place where you feel good about investing a portion of your money in the stock market and to sit back, relax, and watch as your money grows for you over time. Because while there will always be risk in the stock market, and you should never (ever!) put all your money there, there are ways to invest intelligently and safely and ways to feel good about the decisions you make.

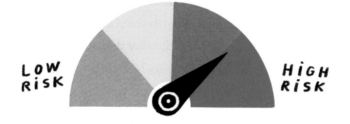

LOW
RISK

HIGH
RISK

A NOTE ON FEES:

Whenever you invest in the stock market, whether you hire a stockbroker or you're doing it all yourself via an app or a brokerage website, there are fees you'll pay for account maintenance, account management, or to complete a trade. Some types of investments may have higher fees than others but can be worth the investment.

Part of your job as an investor—from now until forever—is to decide what's worth it. You have to decide if the company you want to invest in is worth your money, and you have to decide if the fee you're being charged by the brokerage firm is worth the cost. And while most investing fees are usually small and may seem insignificant at first glance, at the end of the year, or over the course of several years, fees can really add up, so finding the best deal you can should always be your goal. When you're in doubt about a fee you're being charged, Google it! The only way to know if you're getting a good deal is to be an informed shopper, and this holds true whether you're shopping for new clothes or the hottest stocks.

WHERE TO PUT YOUR DOUGH TO MAKE iT GROW

At the beginning of this chapter, we talked about how investing is like baking bread. You start with the dough (your money) and then put it in an oven to heat it up. There are three main types of ovens (and with this, we promise we're done with the baking analogy) that have reliably helped people make their fortunes rise over time: stocks (also referred to as equities or generally as the stock market), bonds, and cash equivalents. Here's a rundown on each:

WHAT'S A STOCK?

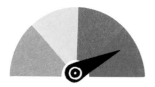

A stock is a small slice of a company's business. When you buy stock in a company, you become a part owner of that business. You're called a shareholder because each portion you buy is called a share. Thousands of companies offer shares for sale to the public—Amazon, Apple, Tesla, Netflix, Whole Foods, Chipotle, Target, Urban Outfitters, the list goes on. (Hint: Just Google "Is [company name] publicly traded?" to find out if you can buy its stock.) There are also fractional shares of stock. If you want to buy a stock with a more expensive price than you can afford, you can buy a fractional share—or slice—at a cheaper price and start investing that way.

How Stocks Work: Stocks are bought and sold (or traded) on stock exchanges like the New York Stock Exchange or the NASDAQ. Shares are priced individually based on the health of the business as well as what other shareholders are willing to pay. If the company does well and the stock price goes up, you make money (called a profit) when you sell your shares. 💥 If the business goes down and drags down the share price with it, when you sell, you lose money. 😠 Each company has a ticker symbol (a three- or four-letter code) that you can track. You may have seen the stocks app on your cell phone before, which allows you to track stock prices and see how your investments are doing. Rather than moving this app to some rarely used folder, why not bring it to the forefront and check in to see how your favorite companies are doing?

Good to Know: Stock prices can swing wildly from day to day, hour by hour, and even minute by minute—and your investment dollars swing right along with them. However, historically over the long term, the stock market has always won, and investors have won with it. The key is to hold on tight when the stock market takes a dive and ride it out. Another way to protect yourself from losses is to spread your money across lots of different investments. This is called diversification, and it basically means that all your investment eggs are not stuck in one basket. When your investments are diversified, you're less exposed to the ups and downs of any single company because you own literally dozens of stocks. So, for example, if one of the tech companies you invested in fails, you won't necessarily lose money because there's a good chance one of the other companies, in a different industry, did well.

WHAT'S A MUTUAL FUND?

A mutual fund is like a variety pack of stocks sold in a single bundle. The stocks in that basket are chosen by a mutual fund manager (a professional stock picker) based on certain criteria, like company size, geography, or potential for growth. A mutual fund is a way to invest in a bunch of stocks at once without having to save up enough money to buy each stock individually. Because a mutual fund allows you to buy several different stocks for different types of companies (technology companies, real estate firms, and retailers, for example), this gives you instant diversification. P.S., Sometimes there are bonds in mutual funds, too. More on that in a sec.

How Mutual Funds Work: When you invest in a mutual fund, your money is pooled with a bunch of other investors. Collectively, that gives the fund manager enough money to buy many shares of dozens of companies at once.

WHY WOULD i WANT TO iNVEST iN A MUTUAL FUND?

If you want diversity in your portfolio, mutual funds can give that to you instantly. Since mutual funds contain a variety of stocks, you won't have to make decisions about which individual stocks to pick out. These funds contain a variety of stocks that have been hand-picked by experts with the expectation that they will earn money over time.

Good to Know: There are thousands of mutual funds to choose from. One easy way to choose is to invest in a target-date mutual fund. A target-date fund is a type of fund with the mix of holdings based on the year an investor (you) wants to retire (as in your target retirement date). As that date draws closer, the mix of investments in the fund is adjusted to give you just the right risk exposure to different types of investments. It's what's known as a set-it-and-forget-it investment.

WHAT'S AN iNDEX FUND?

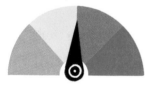

An index fund is a type of mutual fund that contains only companies that are part of a particular stock market index (e.g., the Standard & Poor's 500, which is 500 of the largest US companies; the NASDAQ index, dominated mainly by technology companies; etc.).

How Index Funds Work: Unlike actively managed mutual funds, which are run by people, index funds are run by computer. All of the companies that are part of a particular index are automatically included. And because the companies in an index go up and down in value, the entire index—and the fund that mirrors its holdings—does, too. So when you hear that the S&P is up 2%, your investment in an S&P 500 index fund will also be up 2%.

Why Would I Want to Invest in an Index Fund? When we look at long-term stock market history, index funds have earned more money than other types of mutual funds. Billionaire investor Warren Buffet has said that sticking with these types of funds is a smart investing move for all investors.

Good to Know: Because index funds don't require someone picking and choosing stocks, the management fees investors pay are pretty cheap, which is a good thing for your bottom line!

WHAT'S AN ETF (EXCHANGE-TRADED FUND)?

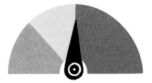

An **ETF** is like a mutual fund (often an index fund) that trades like a stock.

How ETFs Work: ETFs trade on the stock exchanges just like stocks. And like stocks, the price can fluctuate all day when the stock market is open. In comparison, mutual funds don't trade on the exchanges; they can only be bought and sold once per day.

Why Would I Want to Invest in an ETF? Since you can trade ETFs on the same trading platforms that you trade stocks, some people find them easier to invest in. In that way, ETFs give trading flexibility because at the same time you're trading stocks, you can diversify your portfolio by investing in an ETF.

Good to Know: Many mutual funds have a minimum investment requirement (e.g., $500 and up). ETFs offer an inexpensive way to invest in a diversified portfolio one share at a time if you can't afford the cost of admission to a full-sized mutual fund.

WHAT'S A BOND?

You know how when you put your money into savings at a bank, you're basically loaning your money to a bank? That's why they pay you interest. Well, a **bond** is a loan to a corporation or government. It pays you interest (which when we're talking about bonds is called the yield. The amount of your initial investment is called your principal) for allowing that company or government to use your money over a fixed period of time. Bonds are considered a stable investment. They're not going to swing wildly in how much they pay. But in exchange for that stability, history says you're not going to earn as much over time with bonds as with stocks.

To think about that another way, let's return to the topic of risk: There is always a risk/reward component to investing. The more risk you take, the higher the return is likely to be, but the chance to lose money is higher also. Stocks are riskier than bonds and provide a historically higher return. Bonds are safer, and their return is lower. Ideally, you'll have both to help you take just the right amount of risk for you.

How Bonds Work: When you buy a bond, you know how it's going to come out in the end. If you hold the bond for a certain amount of time (called the term), you will get back the money you paid for the bond plus an amount of interest on top.

Good to Know: Your grandparents probably invest most of their money in bonds, but even young people use them to help provide stability in an investment portfolio.

RATES OF RETURN: SHOW ME THE MONEY!

We get it. These definitions are great, but now you're off to the races and you wanna know the really good stuff: How much will I make if I invest my money in any of these assets?

When you hear the phrase "rate of return," which you'll hear often as an investor, that refers to how much an investment grows over a particular time period. Like interest, this rate is measured in percentage terms.

Above we used 10% as an example rate of return just to make the math easy. But—confession time!—rates of return are a bit of a moving target. They change all the time. However, if you average them out over the years, you get a good idea of what to expect from different types of investments. Fun fact: As the average return goes up, so does the amount of risk you take when you buy them. For reference:

- If you keep your money in cash or cash alternatives (e.g., savings accounts, money market accounts, CDs, US Treasury Bills), historically, you can expect to earn anywhere from 0.01% to 1% on your savings. Frankly, the interest you earn in a bank account will barely keep up with inflation. Risk level = none.
- Bonds have historically delivered a higher average rate of return in the 5% to 6% range per year. Risk level = low to medium.
- You'll get the biggest bang for your buck by investing in the stock market. Over roughly the last one hundred years, stocks have shown an annual return of about 10% per year. Risk level = medium and up (but diversification helps!).

YOUR PORTFOLIO AND WHAT'S IN IT

You've seen us mention your investment portfolio a few times now. Don't be intimidated by the term. It's really just a fancy way of saying *all of your investments together*. An investor's portfolio should contain a diversified mix of stocks, bonds, mutual funds, and other assets. When you have a mix of all these assets, you have a diversified portfolio—which is exactly what you want. No one should have all their money invested in one single company in case that company fails. Smart investors know that investing in a lot of different areas and industries and that having a varied portfolio is the best way to earn money in the stock market over time.

If you invested $1 in the year 2000, here's how much it would be worth in 2020:

- If kept in cash, $1 would be worth $1.36 in 2020. However, due to inflation, you'd need $1.48 for it to purchase the same amount.
- If invested in a bond, $1 would be worth $2.50.
- If invested in the stock market, $1 would be worth $3.08.

If $100 was invested from 1990 to 2019:

	Average annual return from 1990–2019	How much $100 would be worth after 30 years	Total Profit
Cash (3-month T-Bill)	2.5%	$205	$105
Cash adjusted for inflation	0.01%	$103	$3
Gold	4.8%	$390	$290
Stock market*	8.2%	$978	$878

As measured by the S&P 500 Stock Index

As you look at that comparison, you may be wondering . . .

WHY NOT INVEST ALL OF MY MONEY IN THE STOCK MARKET?

Because scary.

Stock prices go up and down every day—sometimes dramatically. That is what makes it a risky place to stash *all* of your cash, especially any money you plan to spend soon (tomorrow, next month, even five years from now). However, over longer stretches of time (ten, twenty, or thirty-plus years), stocks have always bounced back from any losses and then some. (Like we mentioned earlier, the historical

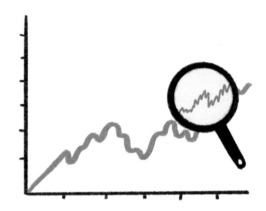

average annual return for stocks is around 10%.) The trick is that you have to be patient and wait out the occasional nausea-inducing drops that make investing sometimes seem like a runaway roller coaster ride.

1 YEAR   5 YEARS   20 YEARS

HOW To iNVEST

And now the moment we've all waited for. It's time to put your savings into action and invest your money! If we knew the song that makes you feel most like conquering the world, we'd be blasting it right now to mark the occasion. Since we don't, we'll just get some administrative stuff out of the way so you can start bragging about becoming a bona fide investor ASAP.

Here's what you'll need:

1. A brokerage account, which may require a parent or adult to sign up for you/with you
2. At least $1 to get started
3. The excitement to dive in and get started ASAP
4. A willingness to stick with it!

1. OPEN A BROKERAGE ACCOUNT

A brokerage account is similar to a bank account except it comes with VIP access to investments like stocks and mutual funds. Most brokerage firms have minimum age requirements. The completely legal work-around here is to have an adult open a custodial brokerage account with you. Although the account will be in their name at first, you'll be able to take full control when you turn eighteen or twenty-one (depending on state laws). If you're already a legal adult, you can open your own brokerage account! Discount brokers like Fidelity, Schwab, or Vanguard; robo advisors like Betterment, Wealthfront, or Ellevest; or apps like Acorns or Robinhood are good places to start.

2. DEPOSIT MONEY

At most brokerages, you don't even need to deposit any money to open an account. But you're going to need to move money into the account when you're ready to invest it. The easiest way is to transfer money from your bank account into your brokerage account, which you can do electronically. Once you deposit money, you can add or withdraw it as well as buy and sell investments within the account. (Note: Your money will automatically be held in cash within your brokerage account when you deposit it or sell out of an investment.)

3. MAKE YOUR FIRST TRADE, ROCK STAR!

You don't need a lot of money to get started investing, especially since most brokerages don't charge trading commissions. All you need is enough to cover the cost of at least one share of the stock or ETF you want to buy.

One share might not sound like much, but it's a very big deal. This is the beginning of your investing journey!

Now this is going to sound controversial, but we're going to put it out there: For your very first investment, it really doesn't matter how much money you invest—because the most important thing is that you're getting started. Nor does it matter exactly *what* you invest in (an individual stock of a company you love or an index mutual fund). What matters is that you simply experience investing and start the compound interest clock as soon as possible. (Check out those charts above for a reminder of why time is your best friend.)

4. LATHER, RINSE, REPEAT

Keep doing what you're doing! Once you buy a share or invest in a mutual fund, just keep adding dollars to feed the compounding machine. That's how investment empires are built . . . and we're not even exaggerating! ♥ (Don't mind us . . . these are tears of joy. We're dabbing our eyes because we love it when we're present for the birth of a new investor!)

RETiREMENT, WHAT?

We get it. Retirement seems like a long way off. And for you, it is . . . But the sooner you think about it, the better. We already talked about the beauty of compound interest and how much your money grows over time . . . That's why whenever you get a real job—meaning a full-time, "adult" job with benefits—you'll want to open a retirement account.

When people talk about having a job with benefits, they mean two things: health benefits (health insurance, which we'll talk about in Chapter 13, page 207) and retirement benefits, like a 401(k) account (which we talk about on page 32).

But if your employer doesn't offer a retirement account, or if you're self-employed, don't fret. You can open an IRA, an individual retirement account, through any brokerage firm. As soon as you have a part-time job with an actual paycheck (since you'll need proper documentation of what you've earned), you can open an IRA or a Roth IRA. A Roth IRA is a type of IRA into which you can invest no more than $6,000 per year. Ideally, when you have an IRA, you'll be investing money for your future that you won't plan to touch until you turn sixty-five. But you can also pull that money out without penalty to buy your first house or pay for school if you need to.

Trust us—you'll want to start investing for retirement as soon as you have the spare funds to do so. That money could make a big, big difference in your future. See pages 116 and 127 for calculations of what small amounts of money can be worth when invested over time.

CRYPTOCURRENCY: A HOT (AND RISKY) COMMODITY

You've probably heard of Bitcoin, but what is it exactly? In the world of Minecraft, there are Minecoins—a digital currency players can use to buy things in the Minecraft world. But as you may know, digital money is no longer just being exchanged in the realm of video games.

Bitcoin is just one type of digital money called cryptocurrency, but there are thousands of others—as well as a growing network of stores and service providers who accept them as a form of payment. (Bitcoin was the first and is still the largest and most popular.)

Cryptocurrency is peer-to-peer money, meaning it is transferred from one person to another in a way similar to how we use cash. Like the internet is powered by a network of servers, cryptocurrencies are powered by a network of computers that are used to create and earn new coins via a complex process called mining. The CliffsNotes version is that new cryptocurrency "coins" are "mined" when computers in that network (aka miners) successfully solve complex math puzzles (like a sudoku but much more difficult!).

Cryptocurrencies can be divided into smaller units like physical money can be broken up into quarters, nickels, dimes, and pennies. While one Bitcoin is worth thousands of dollars, you can buy and send as little as a few cents' worth of Bitcoin.

Cryptocurrencies can be bought and sold via some of the mainstream online stockbrokers, but there are also crypto-only exchanges (e.g., Coinbase). To store cryptocurrency, you'll need to set up a special digital wallet. It's like a bank vault you can keep either online or via a small, encrypted portable device.

It is important to note that cryptocurrencies are *very* unpredictable, *very* risky investments. This market is still relatively new and cryptocurrency wallets are incredibly attractive targets for hackers. So be warned that these assets are definitely not for inexperienced investors!

However, there's no denying that cryptocurrencies are an interesting, innovative investment and form of money. Certain athletes have begun receiving portions of their salaries in cryptocurrency and major corporations are starting to accept Bitcoin as a form of payment for their goods and services. If you're curious to learn more about the technology and ideas behind cryptocurrencies, check out Bitcoin.org.

HOW CRYPTO WORKS

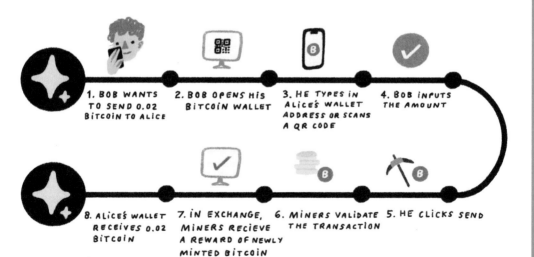

1. BOB WANTS TO SEND 0.02 BITCOIN TO ALICE

2. BOB OPENS HIS BITCOIN WALLET

3. HE TYPES IN ALICE'S WALLET ADDRESS OR SCANS A QR CODE

4. BOB INPUTS THE AMOUNT

8. ALICE'S WALLET RECEIVES 0.02 BITCOIN

7. IN EXCHANGE, MINERS RECIEVE A REWARD OF NEWLY MINTED BITCOIN

6. MINERS VALIDATE THE TRANSACTION

5. HE CLICKS SEND

HOW TO INVEST $100,000 WITHOUT LOSING A DIME

Stock market simulators (like the Investopedia Stock Market Game) let you practice virtual trading without putting a single dollar on the line. They're sometimes called paper trading accounts and often look exactly like the real brokerage platform available in real life. Go ahead and make some big-dollar bets and see what happens!

HOW TO INVEST IN CAUSES YOU BELIEVE IN

If what you buy is a reflection of your values, then the same can be said of what you invest in.

Socially responsible investing (SRI) (also called sustainable, responsible impact investing) is a way to align your money with the causes and issues you care most about. One of the easiest ways to invest with your conscience is to buy an SRI mutual fund. To pick the companies held in the mutual fund, the fund managers screen for stocks that meet certain criteria, such as a company's environmental or governance record, social impact, industry of operation (e.g., green technology), and other factors (you may also hear these funds referred to as ESG investments for environmental, social, governance). Another way to reflect your beliefs in your portfolio is to buy shares in individual companies that you admire for the way they run their business. There are also investment firms that put together mini-portfolios of stocks and ETFs based on particular themes.

THE FIRE MOVEMENT: FINANCIAL INDEPENDENCE, RETIRE EARLY

How does it sound to be able to quit a job you hate, retiring as soon as you can? Devotees of the FIRE Movement not only say it's possible, they've also actually done it.

What's the FIRE Movement? It stands for Financial Independence, Retire Early. People who buy into this way of life spend a chunk of years saving a huge percentage of their income (often 50–70% of whatever they're bringing in) with a goal of quitting their day jobs in order to do something they find more fulfilling. They do this by living extremely frugally, sometimes adding side-gigs so they can earn more and then save more in a rapid-fire way.

Do They Really Not Work From the Time They're Thirty or Forty until—Well—Ever? Ehh. FIRE fans will tell you the emphasis is more on the "FI" than the "RE." The goal is to no longer have to spend your days doing something you're not passionate about—because it pays you—but instead to be able to have more freedom, more choices. You can spend more time traveling, more time with family, or transition into a job that you love (but that might not pay quite so well) because you've got money to back you up.

How Does This Work, By the Numbers? FIRE math is actually very specific. You are said to have achieved financial independence when you've saved 25 times your annual expenses. This works because of something called the 4% rule. That's an assumption that if you invest the money you've saved in a diversified portfolio, you should be able to withdraw 4-ish% of it a year pretty much indefinitely. So . . . once you've saved 25 times your yearly expenses, that 4% equals one year of expenses—enough to live on.

Is This for You? Even if it's not, there's a lot to learn from the FIRE Movement for people who want to live a financial life that's under their control. It focuses on how much you spend, how much you save, and how both of those things are well within your control. It also shows you just how powerful supercharging your saving rate can be. Last point here: FIRE is designed to provide an escape from the day job you don't particularly like, but there's nothing bad about work. Working, staying busy, and involving yourself in an activity is always a good thing. It keeps us healthy and social, and it's generally associated with a happier life.

TL;DR

CHAPTER 8 KEY TAKEAWAYS

- When you're investing, you're putting your money to work to make *more money*. Think of investing in the stock market like baking bread. You put your dough in the oven (aka your money in the stock market), turn it to the right temperature (aka choose your investments), and eventually it will bake into a delicious loaf (aka grow into a sizable investment you can be proud of). The oven (aka the stock market) does most of the work.

- We invest for two big reasons—to stay ahead of inflation (which zaps the purchasing power from your money) and to harness the power of compound interest (where our interest earns interest on itself and builds wealth).

- We're telling you about the power of investing now because starting early is what makes all the difference in your financial future. The more time you have to let your money grow (thanks, compound interest!), the more you'll earn over the course of your lifetime. So get to it!

- There are many different types of investments you can make. There's stock, which is a small slice of a company's business. There are mutual funds, which are like a variety pack of stocks sold in a single bundle. There are bonds, which is a loan to a corporation or government, that pay interest to you. And that's just for starters.

- Don't get freaked out, but one of these days, you're gonna lose money. All investors do. Stock prices go up and down every day—sometimes dramatically. Over longer stretches of time (ten, twenty, thirty, or more years), stocks have always bounced back from their losses and earn investors an average of 10% annually. The trick is being patient. Slow. And. Steady. Wins. The. Race.

SANDRA LOPEZ

VICE PRESIDENT AND GENERAL MANAGER OF INTEL SPORTS

WHICH WORDS DEFINE YOU?

Perpetual student, resilient, passionate.

WHAT'S YOUR JOB?

I lead a team responsible for business development and product marketing in the media and sports industry.

WHAT'S THE CHANGE YOU'RE LOOKING TO CREATE IN THE WORLD?

That all women should have a seat at the C-level and on a board of directors if they want it. I'm with Ruth Bader Ginsburg, who said that she wouldn't be satisfied until there were nine women on the Supreme Court. We shouldn't settle for anything less than 100%.

TELL US ABOUT YOUR FIRST JOB.

I started my career in fashion as a fashion buyer. My salary was $35,000, and that was in 1995.

WHAT'S THE BIGGEST MONEY MISTAKE YOU EVER MADE?

Whenever I got a bonus from my employer, I would spend that money on a reward for my hard work. But I wish I'd had a better understanding of what my bigger financial goals were and what I needed to save. I wish I had run my personal finances as if my household were a business.

WHAT'S THE SMARTEST MONEY MOVE YOU EVER MADE?

I am thankful that I made a financial plan with a financial wealth manager who was able to give me an understanding of where every dime of my money was going and what I needed to do to ensure financial security.

TELL US A MONEY STORY THAT MADE YOU WHO YOU ARE TODAY.

There are things in your life that will completely change the dynamics of how you manage your money like getting a divorce or taking a new job. The challenge is accepting those changes and having the discipline to forge a new and improved path in your financial life.

WHAT ONE PIECE OF CAREER ADVICE WOULD YOU GIVE TO YOUR YOUNGER SELF?

For years, I was taught to "fit in; don't stand out," but I realized that when I did this, I wasn't giving the company I worked for 100% because I was not being my authentic self. Don't be afraid to embrace your uniqueness—that is an asset that will help you grow in your career.

WHAT ONE PIECE OF MONEY ADVICE WOULD YOU GIVE TO YOUR YOUNGER SELF?

Don't be afraid to talk about money with your friends and family because it makes you more confident and knowledgeable.

WHAT ARE THE TOP THREE THINGS YOU THINK EVERY FIRST-TIME INVESTOR NEEDS TO KNOW TO GET STARTED ON HER INVESTING/SAVING JOURNEY?

1. Understand where every dime is going. You need transparency with your money.

2. Take your financial life as seriously as you take your work life. Your money should be treated with the same respect as your career.

3. Know what your aspirations are. Do you want to save $1 million? Do you want to travel the world? Make sure your financial life is in line with your values.

TO-DO LIST FOR PART 2:

Congrats! You completed part 2, and we're doing the dance of joy over here at HerMoney HQ. What's your next step? Put some of this section's most important takeaways into action with the following . . .

Write Down a Goal You Have and Research How Much It Might Cost. For example, a weekend away with your friends. How much money do you think it will cost to take this trip? Make a list of your expected expenses like travel, hotels, meals, and entertainment to give yourself a general idea. When you get the total, figure out exactly how much you'll need to save before the date approaches. Then you can break that figure down by week into bite-sized savings goals.

Getting Banked. Congrats! If you're ready to open a bank account, know that you'll need to do it jointly with your parent or legal guardian until you hit age eighteen. At that point you can open the account in your name alone. Gather everything you'll need:

❏ Two forms of ID—like a driver's license, passport, or birth certificate (these can be from the adult opening the account with you)

❏ An initial deposit to put into the account.

It may take you a few weeks to save enough money for your initial deposit. That's okay. The important thing is that you're getting started on your banking journey!

Change the World . . . with Your Dollars. One (pretty dang incredible) thing about becoming an investor is that when you own a stock, you own a piece of the company you invest in. This means that your dollars can help shape the world you want to live in. For example, if you're passionate about environmental justice, you can invest in a company that helps clean up waterways and streams. Or if you're passionate about animal rights, you can invest in a company that's pioneering plant-based meat substitutes. There are countless ways you can make a difference in the world when you invest.

Take a sheet of paper. On one side, make a list of at least three causes you're most passionate about. On the other side, leave room to list several publicly traded companies (companies that you can buy shares of on the stock market) that help elevate awareness of those causes or bring about change. Where to find this information? Google will be your best friend. For example, you can Google "companies saving the planet" or search for "socially conscious investing lists." Take a look around and see where you might want to put your money when the time comes. Even if you don't have the funds to invest right now, you can start tracking these companies' stock and see how they perform over time.

PART 3

USE IT

9

SPENDING SMART

You Don't Need It, and You Might Not Even Really Want It—So Why Did You Feel Compelled to Buy It? (We Know; We've Done It, Too)

We'd all like to be able to say yes to everything we want to do, but there are only so many hours of the day, days of the week, weeks in the year, and years in a lifetime available to us to do everything on our list. So we prioritize—putting things at the top of the list that we want most. Everything else moves lower.

Managing money works the same way. We have a limited amount of it, which means we have to prioritize what we want to spend it on. At the same time, there are a lot of outside forces (retailers, marketers, peers, social media) doing their best to convince you to spend more money on things that aren't even on your list.

A big part of the challenge is . . .

IMPULSE CONTROL: WHY IT'S SO HARD TO STICK TO YOUR SHOPPING LIST

S-A-L-E. That's a beautiful word, isn't it? Our brains think so. They can't resist a bargain. Seriously, there's an entire area of scientific study behind what makes us buy stuff.

Back in the 1970s, a researcher named Paco Underhill wrote

a book called *Why We Buy: The Science of Shopping*. It contained lots of observations about shoppers in the wild, wild world of retail. To this day, retailers rely on this science to make us give in to our spending impulses. For example, your height. What does how tall you are have to do with the brand of cereal you buy? A lot, it turns out.

After observing countless hours of customers shopping, behavioral scientists noted that people didn't spend much time looking at higher and lower shelves. They tended to purchase products displayed at eye level. So grocers started placing the cereal they *wanted* customers to buy at eye level and moving the less expensive choices to lower or higher shelves. And that's not all. Did you know:

- Shoppers tend to turn to the right after entering a store. Note how stores are arranged to steer you through as many of the aisles of merchandise as possible.
- Samples (of food, a new lotion, or colors of lip gloss) and the ability to touch items leads to more buying.
- When we see a sign that says SALE!, we assume we're getting a bargain even if the price hasn't actually changed. Before you get excited about getting a deal, do the math. A 10% sale on a $20 item means you're only saving $2.
- The buy-two-get-one-free trap: We may only need one makeup brush, but who can resist getting a freebie? Not us (usually). We end up spending more to get freebies we often never use.

So the next time you're in a store, note the background music, wall color, ultra-flattering lighting, and how employees greet you. All of it is designed to inspire you to spend, spend, spend.

ONLiNE SHOPPiNG: NEW TRiCKS, SAME RESULTS

The same types of things happen online, where every click pattern is mapped out in painstaking detail. E-tailers know how you got from the home page to the sale sections of novelty socks and how many other online shoppers took the same path. They're measuring which pop-up ad works best, whether people are more likely to click the green or blue button, and on and on. Every single advertisement that has ever inspired you to buy was designed to get you to do *exactly that*.

Don't feel bad if you've fallen for temptations and ended up overspending. Our brains are just wired that way. The problem is that once we get that endorphin rush from buying something new, it's not long until we revert to our set happy place and crave that buzz again. It's like being on a treadmill that you can't stop or slow down. (In fact, the phenomenon is technically called the hedonic treadmill.)

But you can beat this. Just knowing that you're being actively *sold to* can help you with your impulse control.

WATCH OUT FOR "INVISIBLE" MONEY

Advances in technology have also made it easy—wayyy too easy—to spend.

Back in the day, people always paid for things using good old-fashioned cash. Then came credit cards and debit cards and payment apps like Venmo, Zelle, and Apple Pay. We swipe, wave, and send money without ever touching it. On top of that, some of the more socially designed payment apps (looking at you, Venmo!) give us a real-time feed of all the fun stuff our friends—and friends of friends—are spending money on. Cue FOMO.

All of it makes spending money extremely convenient—and easy to lose track of how many dollars you're handing over. Why? Part-ing with actual, physical money snaps our brains to attention. It pains us to fork over the dollar bills at the cash register. But the more removed you are from actual cash, the less your brain registers the fact that you're spending. When you plunk down a credit card or use a payment app, it doesn't have the same impact. We don't feel as much pain when it's invisible money disappearing.

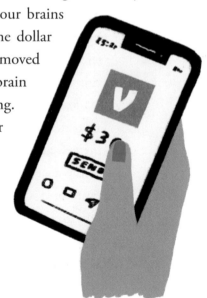

Casinos figured this out a long time ago. They have people exchange their money for plastic chips precisely to dis-tance gamblers from the feeling that they're betting real money. And what do gamblers do? They bet a lot more money than they intended to. The same thing happens with credit cards: Studies have shown that we are willing to spend more (up to 83% more!) when we pay for things with a credit or debit card versus cash.

YOU VS. TECHNOLOGY: HOW TO NOT OVERSPEND

No need to delete the payment apps from your phone or cut up your credit/debit cards. Here are three ways to outsmart the technology that's urging you to spend mindlessly:

1. **Remove Stored Credit Card Information from Your Apps.** E-tailers know that getting you through the checkout process faster makes it less likely you'll stop and think twice about what you're buying. You can take back control! Delete all that stored payment information, and you'll be forced to manually re-enter all of your details before you click buy. Inconvenient? Yup. But it's also a great way to slow things down so you can think about whether you really want what's in your shopping cart.

2. **Activate Credit/Debit Card Text Alerts.** Many credit and debit cards, budget trackers, and apps allow you to set alarms that are triggered 1) if your card balance goes above a certain level or the amount in your account falls below a certain amount, 2) if your spending on a certain category (e.g., clothes or puppy toys) goes above an amount you set, or 3) if you make any purchase that's more than a set dollar amount.

3. **Carry a Reminder of Your Goals.** Remember that being able to visualize your goals helps you stay on track.

So create a living reminder—a photograph of the Eiffel Tower if your goal is to study abroad, for example—and make it your wallpaper on your phone screen. It will help you keep all other spending temptations in context.

SEVEN WAYS TO CURB THE URGE TO SPLURGE

1. **Shop with a List.** Yes, it's old fashioned. But it works. If it's not on the list, don't buy it.

2. **Press Pause before Unplanned Purchases.** Try this experiment: The next time you see something that you ABSOLUTELY MUST HAVE THIS VERY MOMENT, stop. Wait twenty-four hours. Chances are good the urge will fade away.

3. **Abandon Your Shopping Cart.** This will give you a cooling-off period. Plus, for things you really do want, waiting often also results in a coupon showing up in your inbox from the site you were browsing. Check your email.

4. **Use Cash.** We know. Sounds so 1999. But cash can keep your spending in line the way credit cards and payment apps can't. You are physically limiting your ability to make extra purchases to the cash you have with you. P.S., Carrying bills in large denominations helps. They're harder to let go of.

5. **Think in Hours Not Dollars.** Translate the price of everything you think of buying into the hours it would cost to earn that

money. For example, if you have a job that pays $10 an hour, you'd have to work six hours to pay for a $60 pair of shoes. Still want them? We didn't think so.

6. **Don't Shop at the End of the Day.** You may have heard how you're not supposed to go grocery shopping when you're hungry. It's harder to resist impulse food purchases on an empty stomach. You shouldn't go when you're tired either—e.g., at the end of the day. It's harder to avoid temptation.

7. **Give Yourself an "Oops" Allowance.** We're all allowed the occasional slip-up. Set aside a specific amount you can safely allow yourself to spend each week on completely and totally unplanned purchases (as in "Oops, this wasn't on the list!"). If you don't spend it all, roll over the amount to the following week.

OOPSY ALLOWANCE

WHAT A SMART SHOPPER YOU ARE!

We're surprised that comparison shopping hasn't become an official Olympic sport. There's a growing number of blogs, online tools, and mobile apps to help shoppers compare prices, snag coupons, and get an alert when an item goes on sale. Here are some ways to make sure you're getting the best price possible—and lessen your environmental footprint as a consumer:

- **Comparison Shop IRL and Online at the Same Time.** Your phone makes it easy to check prices on the items you're checking out at a store. Some apps make it as easy as snapping a picture in your search bar to scan the barcode.
- **Set Price Alerts.** Browser extensions (like Honey, Camelcamel-camel, and others) allow you to see the price history of items on

Amazon and other large e-commerce sites to find the best deals. You can also set an alert to tell you when there's a price drop.

- **Search for Coupons.** Googling a retailer's name and the words "coupon code" before checkout will usually bring you an online code to plug in at checkout. Ka-ching.

WHO NEEDS NEW?

Not us! Buying used is the retail version of recycling. You'll save the planet and save money at the same time. Plus it feels like a treasure hunt. What's not to love? Here's

a look at some of the ways the Her-Money team loves to go the vintage and consignment route.

CONSIGNMENT: Hiring another person or company to sell your belongings (like clothing or furniture) you no longer want. They pay you after the merch sells and keep a portion of the proceeds as a fee.

Shop Secondhand. Thrift stores, resale/ consignment shops like ThreadUp and Poshmark, Craigslist, Freecycle, Buy Nothing groups, Facebook Marketplace, NextDoor . . . all these sites/apps together present a shopping mall's worth of gently used (sometimes new) items. And they're not just for buying. Selling your lightly used stuff can yield big bucks.

Host a Swap Party. Ask your friends to clean out their closets and then invite them over. The admission fee? A couple of bags of unwanted clothes, shoes, and accessories they're willing to pass on to others. You can even expand the circle of swapping by having each person invite a friend.

Rent It: There are some events that require a special big-ticket outfit for just one night (prom, a wedding, a spring formal). If borrowing from someone isn't an option, you can look to rent through a service like Rent the Runway. Added bonus: When you rent, you won't feel guilty about completely changing looks for the next gig. Plus, renting and all of the options on this list are super sustainable. You're getting away from fast fashion and that's a great thing.

HOW TO ASK FOR A BETTER DEAL

You'd be surprised how much wiggle room there is on goods and services. Here's how to ask for a discount whether you're negotiating rent, a new phone, your cable bill, or anything, really. Plus, there are often "student discounts" for people just like you.

Thank the Salesperson or Customer Service Rep in Advance. Ask yourself how you'd want to be treated if you were in their shoes. Now act that way.

Say, "Thank you so much for helping me out; I'm so glad to be talking to you. Let me fill you in on the situation." Then give them some details about why you're calling and what you're hoping they can help you with.

Research Competitor Prices Beforehand. Use that dollar

amount (or 10–20% less) as your negotiation goal. To show that you've done your research, politely mention your research on rates.

Say, "I saw that [X company] is currently extending offers of [$X or $X per month]. I'd like to be paying the same."

Ask for a Walk-Through of your Bill. If you're an existing customer (maybe calling your cell phone company to ask for a discount), ask the customer service rep to explain what you're paying for. (This is also a good way to see if there are any services you can drop.)

Say, "I'm not certain I understand all of the line items on my bill. Can you please walk me through them so I can know how it adds up to so much?"

Ask about Flexibility. You want to invite a discussion, not lay out a demand.

Say, "I'm wondering if there's flexibility to bring that amount down—is that something you can help me with?"

If you strike out, you might simply be speaking with someone who doesn't have the power to grant you a discount. Ask *nicely* to speak to someone else (a supervisor, perhaps) who might have the authority to help you out.

TL;DR

CHAPTER 9 KEY TAKEAWAYS

- Money is a limited resource—which means we can't buy everything. Spending time setting priorities will help us accomplish our financial (and life!) goals—both large and small.
- If you're ready to curb the urge to splurge, we've got seven ways to do it: shop with a list, press pause before making unplanned purchases, abandon your shopping cart (when shopping online), go on a cash-only diet, think in hours not dollars, don't shop late in the day, and give yourself an allowance for the occasional spending slip-up.
- Saving money and saving the planet? Sign us up! We love to shop secondhand at thrift stores, consignment shops, and flea markets. We also love hosting clean-out-the-closet swap parties and using fashion resale apps when we're looking for something more specific than we can find while browsing our local Salvation Army or Goodwill.
- Negotiating is not just for job interviews—you can negotiate for many of the things you spend money on, too.

AMANDA
CLAYMAN

FINANCIAL THERAPIST

WHICH WORDS DEFINE YOU?

Optimistic, empathetic, perceptive, hand-talker.

WHAT'S YOUR JOB?

I'm a clinical social worker who practices as a financial therapist. I went into the mental health field specifically because I wanted to help people address and explore the role of money in their lives.

WHAT'S THE CHANGE YOU'RE LOOKING TO CREATE IN THE WORLD?

To connect people to a more personal, holistic understanding of their money instead of the long list of "I should do this" or "I feel bad about that" judgments and assumptions that most of us have internalized.

TELL US ABOUT YOUR FIRST JOB.

When I moved to New York after college, I got a job as the assistant to the creative director of a nightclub at $25,000 a year. I felt a lot of pressure to fit in with the beautiful people who surrounded me, and that was the beginning of years of struggling with credit card debt.

WHAT'S THE BIGGEST MONEY MISTAKE YOU EVER MADE?

I had such a significant crash and fail around money that it changed my whole life! Money made me so anxious I would avoid the regular tasks of just keeping track of spending or planning for when bills were due.

Despite my constant worry, my debt just seemed to climb. But once I finally ran out of ways to deny the debt, I looked to fix the problem.

WHAT'S THE SMARTEST MONEY MOVE YOU EVER MADE?

I learned from failure. I avoided dealing with my debt problem for a long time, but once I did, I was shocked by how much I learned about myself.

TELL US A MONEY STORY THAT MADE YOU WHO YOU ARE TODAY.

When I was twenty-six, my mom visited me in New York. I asked her if she would cut my hair. She gave me a truly terrible style, and when I burst into tears, she tried to reassure me by saying we could call my hairstylist and tell her it was an emergency. That just made me cry harder because I had to admit to her that the last time I got my hair cut, I had paid with a check that had bounced so I couldn't go back. My mom simply asked, "Don't you have a budget?" and when I admitted that I didn't, she showed me how to create one.

WHAT ONE PIECE OF CAREER ADVICE WOULD YOU GIVE TO YOUR YOUNGER SELF?

Follow your curiosity. I've always believed that I can learn from each job and situation, and I can use that learning to continue charting an authentic, fulfilling path.

WHAT ONE PIECE OF MONEY ADVICE WOULD YOU GIVE TO YOUR YOUNGER SELF?

Find your money challenges interesting. Look at them as ways to get to know yourself.

WHAT THREE THINGS DOES EVERY TEEN NEED TO UNDERSTAND ABOUT THEIR BRAIN, THEIR MONEY, AND HOW THEY WORK TOGETHER?

1. Shopping provides a mood boost, but there's usually a post-purchase mood crash.

2. Money is linked to our sense of survival, so when we feel like our financial stability is being threatened, we go right into fight, flight, or freeze mode.

3. When we feel anxious about money, it's our brain's way of signaling that something needs attention. Listen to that feeling, then make a plan to find a calm time and place to investigate the problem and figure out what needs to be done.

10

BiG—TiCKET iTEMS

Your First Car and First Apartment Are Closer than You Think

YOUR FiRST CAR

Buying your own car may seem way out there in the future. It's not as far off as you think. Many people believe they'll buy or lease their first set of wheels at age twenty-one—but it often happens sooner. The earlier you understand the cost involved, the easier it will be for you to get prepped when you're ready.

Some things are obvi. A brand-new Tesla will cost way more than a used Toyota Prius. But other things—like how to research cars, how to negotiate for them, and how to pay for them—are less so.

A FEW RULES OF THE, AHEM, ROAD

First, used is a better value than new. A car's value depreciates—or goes down—by 20–30% by the time it's a year old, and it continues to lose about 12% a year after that. However, because the average lifespan of a car is now about twelve years, a used car between three to five years old has a long time to run. That's where the sweet spot is when

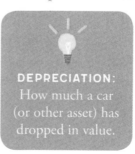

DEPRECIATION:
How much a car (or other asset) has dropped in value.

you're looking for your first car. The lower the mileage, the better. The older a car is, the more likely it is to need costly repairs.

That said, you'll have to do your research. If you're buying used, you'll need to look up the estimated value of the car on Kelley Blue Book (KBB), Edmunds, or another site that specializes in giving the valuations for used cars. With a used car, you'll also need to make sure the car has never been in a serious accident. A search of your potential car's VIN—or vehicle identification number—on CARFAX or Auto-Check should tell you everything you need to know.

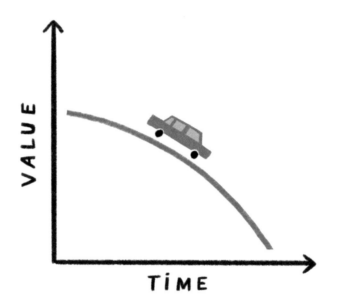

Remember, the cost of a car isn't just the cost of your car payment. There will be insurance, gas, and maintenance. Depending on where you live, you may have to pay for a place to park it. Add all of these costs up then compare with the cost (and convenience) of using public transportation or even frequent rideshares in your area before you make the decision to become a car owner. Rule of thumb: Don't spend more than 15% of your monthly take-home amount on transportation.

HOW TO BUY IN THREE STEPS

Step 1: Before You Even Step Foot into a Car Dealer, Hit the Internet. It is filled with quality information about pretty much every car on the planet. Chances are, you have at least some idea of what kind of car you want—maybe a small SUV, electric, or hybrid—and what your budget looks  like. That's a very good start. With just those two pieces of information, you can begin clicking.

Eventually, you'll settle into a price range, but you should know that the prices you see listed at the dealership aren't final. Cars go on sale just like other things, but these sales come in the form of incentives and rebates. A rebate is a certain amount of money you might get back for buying a particular car. An incentive doesn't have to be cash. It can be a low-interest-rate loan when you buy the car—in commercials you may have heard the words "0% financing." That's an incentive.

Step 2: Now It's Time to Go Shopping. You can and should go to a dealer because that's the place to test drive different models, both new and used. Drive the specific model with the features that are most important to you so you can try them out. If it's a used car, carefully examine it inside and out. When you drive any car, you'll want to accelerate (take it on the highway if you can), turn, and brake. Finally, if it's not a certified used car (which means the manufacturer has thor-

oughly tested it and is providing an additional warranty), bring in an independent mechanic to inspect it. It's worth the cost.

Don't feel like you have to make a deal on your first trip to the dealership. You should take all the information you get and then use it to shop around for the same car both online and off. If you're buying new, the number to look at is called the MSRP, the Manufacturer's Suggested Retail Price, which you can find online. Then aim to pay 10–12% less. And when the salesperson starts offering extended warranties and other add-ons? Just say no. You can always buy them later. There's no need for that sort of pressure now.

Let's talk haggling and negotiating for a minute. Should you do it? Absolutely! One way to do it is to find similar cars from different dealers. Get the best price you can from one, then ask the others if they can beat it. The best time to shop for a car is near the end of the month and near the end of the year. That's because salespeople have sales goals to meet, so they are more willing to make a deal.

If you're buying from another person, you still have to do all the research—and make sure that you can test drive the car. But there are differences: For one, you'll need to have all the money up front. Also, they're not going to be able to give you a warranty, so all repairs and maintenance costs will be on you. On the upside, there are no dealer fees (these can run up to $1,000 on the transaction), and there probably won't be as much pushy sales talk. If you like the car after your test drive, make an appointment with a trusted mechanic. Have them inspect the vehicle and let you know if it's in good shape. One very important thing to look for when you're buying from another person is a clean title, or ownership papers, that lists the seller as the owner of this car outright (with no financing), giving that person the right to sell it to you. If there's still a loan on the car or there is no title, walk away.

Step 3: Pay for It.

Most people need a loan to pay for a car—new or used. This is one of the reasons you want to build and maintain good credit. Car dealerships and online car sites will offer you financing, but don't take it before you shop around.

Unless you know that the car you want has a financing deal, you're going to want to look at car loans from banks and credit unions. Credit unions, in particular, are known for offering really good interest rates on used car loans. To find the best rates, go to a site like BankRate.com and search car loans (new or used).

Once you find a good rate—from a credit union, bank, or a car dealer—you have to go through an application process. That means your credit will be checked, and based on your score, you will be offered a particular interest rate. If you suspect that you'll want to get your own financing, obtaining it before you go into a car dealer or before you start shopping online is a good idea because it gives you a better sense of how much you can afford to spend on the car itself. Note: No one says you have to spend as much as they'll lend you. It's perfectly fine— better even—to spend much less.

SAMPLE CAR BUDGET

INSURANCE

DEPRECIATION

GAS

MAINTENANCE

LICENSE/ REGISTRATION/ TAXES

TIRES

Let's say you want to spend $15,000 total on a car and to pay it off over the course of five years. Five years (or sixty months) is the average length of a car loan. The average auto loan interest rate hovers around 5%. For a $13,000 car paid off over five years with a loan at 5% interest, you'll end up paying around $245 per month or $14,720 total. (Yep, that additional $1,720 is the interest you pay.)

But let's say you want your monthly payments to be lower, and the dealership offers you a chance to extend your loan to seven years, or eighty months, and pay just $184 per month. At first glance, this might seem like an appealing option, but the longer you take to pay off the loan, the more you end up paying in interest. With this example, you'd end up paying $15,434 for your car or $2,434 in interest—and you'd go over your initial budget. It's important to be absolutely sure that you plan on keeping the car at least as long as it will take to pay it off!

If you can't get financing yourself because you don't have enough (or good enough) credit history, you can ask a parent (or someone else) to co-sign for you. When someone acts as a co-signer on a loan for you, they're vouching for you to pay back the loan. In order for you to qualify for the loan, you are using *their* credit score and *their* good financial standing. Which also means if you miss a payment or don't pay the loan, it reflects on them, and they become responsible for making the payment. Co-signing is not something to take lightly—by you or by your co-signer. If you are lucky enough to get a co-signer, make sure to protect the relationship, and the loan, by paying it off each month.

INSURANCE, TAXES, TITLES, AND FEES

No matter what kind of car you get, you're going to need car insurance. Car insurance covers everything from the tow trucks and car repairs you might need in the event of an accident to any medical care you or other drivers or passengers involved in a wreck might need. There are many factors that affect how much you'll pay for car insurance, including where you live, the car you drive, and how old you are. But it's not cheap. On average, an eighteen-year-old female pays about $7,000 a year (that's three times as much as older people pay). One way to bring the cost down is to put the car on your family's insurance policy, even if you have to cover it separately. That costs an average of $2,000 a year.

Taxes, too, vary based on where you live. You'll pay anywhere from nothing in state sales tax (in Delaware, New Hampshire, Oregon, and Montana) to as much as 11.5% if you're in Oklahoma, for example.

Finally, you'll also pay fees, including a vehicle registration fee—the more your car costs or weighs, the more expensive it will be to register it. This fee includes all the costs to assign a title and order license plates.

YOUR FIRST PLACE

Just as getting your first car is a major deal, it's a huge step to move out and live on your own—there are no more curfews and there's no one telling you to go to class, to eat dinner, or to make your bed. But it can also be intimidating, especially when it comes to the financial side. Getting a place of your own means getting bills of your own. Bills for rent, utilities, cable, internet, water, and maybe other things. It's one big step into Adultville. So let's help you get prepared to take it.

HOW MUCH SHOULD YOU SPEND?

You may be paying for your first apartment on your own, or someone (like your parents or other family) may be helping you. The rule of thumb is to spend no more than 35% of your monthly income on housing costs. This isn't just rent; it includes your utilities, too. If your parents are chipping in, this may allow you to spring for a more expensive place. Just make sure you understand how long they plan to provide this extra cushion—if there's a deadline, you'll want to take that into consideration when you apartment hunt. You may also look for other ways to bring the cost down: Hello, roomie!

OFTEN OVERLOOKED EXPENSES WHEN FIRST LIVING ON YOUR OWN

Mom and Dad footed the bill for a lot of things that you'll now need to add to your monthly or annual budget. Here's a look:

Toiletries
Cleaning supplies
Makeup
Furniture
Decor (curtains, art, posters, etc.)
Pots, pans, and kitchen supplies
Laundry supplies (detergent, fabric softener, dryer sheets, and quarters in case you have to trek to the laundromat)
Linens (sheets, bedding, towels, etc.)

APPLYING FOR AN APARTMENT

To rent an apartment, you'll need to fill out an application with a landlord or with a leasing company. It'll typically ask for your birth date and Social Security Number so they can run a credit check (ahh, there's that credit again) as well as proof of income. Many landlords require their renters to earn a minimum income—sometimes they even have a formula, such as 40 times the

monthly rent. This means that if you want to rent an apartment that costs $1,000 per month, you'll need to earn at least $40,000 per year.

This can be a problem when you're just starting out. If you don't hit the mark income-wise, or if you have little or no credit history at all (for more on credit history, check page 99!), you'll need a parent or guardian to co-sign the lease.

As with the car loan, when someone co-signs a lease for you, you are still responsible for paying your monthly rent, but they are vouching for you to pay your bills on time. If you miss your monthly rent payment, your landlord can come after your co-signer to pay your bills. And, if you pay late or leave your apartment with money owed on the lease, it can damage your co-signer's credit. So, again, being responsible and respectful is the least you can do!

BEFORE SIGNING A LEASE

When you rent an apartment, you're going to be asked to sign a lease, which is basically a contract you make with the building owner or property manager to pay your rent on time, follow certain rules, and leave the property in the same condition that you received it.

Make sure you read all the fine print—and that you know the answer to these questions:

- How long is the lease for?
- What happens if I need to move and get out of the lease early?
- Will I be charged a fee if I accidentally pay my rent late? If so, how much is it?
- What am I responsible for paying in addition to rent—like gas, electric, garbage pick-up, etc.? These are often called utilities.

- How much is the security deposit?
- How much will you be charged if there is any damage when you move out?
- Are pets allowed? Is there an additional pet fee to have a pet?

Before you sign any lease, make sure to have a parent or another trusted adult review it with you, and before you move into a place, take pictures of all the rooms and document any pre-existing damage (even small damage) so you aren't charged for any damages when you move out. Sometimes, if there are damages, your landlord can elect to keep your security deposit, and you definitely want to get that back!

INSURING YOUR RENTAL (AND ALL YOUR STUFF!)

Just like you need health insurance to cover you in the event of an illness and car insurance to cover you in case of an accident, you need renter's insurance to cover your stuff in case of a break-in, fire, or other disaster. The good news is, it's pretty inexpensive and usually just a couple hundred dollars. With renter's insurance, you'll have either a monthly, quarterly, or annual payment as well as a deductible you'll need to pay (probably a few hundred dollars) before insurance kicks in. When choosing a policy, make sure your coverage includes full replacement value for your things (rather than cash-value coverage, which will pay you back much less). Take photographs or videos of all your possessions (especially valuables like computers, jewelry, and art) so you have proof of ownership. And if you have a lot of electronics or jewelry, make sure you have enough insurance for those things specifically. If you don't, you can buy an add-on policy called a **rider**.

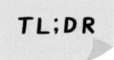

TL;DR

CHAPTER 10 KEY TAKEAWAYS

- Make a list of what you want in a car. Think about both practical things (like low mileage, good safety features, and a warranty) and think about the nice-to-have features like heated seats. Take your list with you whenever you go to shop for a car, so you'll know exactly what you're looking for.
- If you're buying a used car, spend some time on sites like Kelley Blue Book (KBB) and Edmunds, looking up valuations of used cars. How much are the kinds of cars you like going for? It's important to look at pricing before you shop so you'll know if you're getting a good deal.
- Shopping for a car's financing is as important as shopping around for the car itself.
- Don't spend more than 35% of your monthly income on housing.
- You've heard it a thousand times: "Safety first." But it's true. While saving money and getting a good deal on an apartment is amazing, you should prioritize living in a safe, walkable neighborhood over getting a bargain. Sometimes, to get the security you need, you might have to pay a little more for your housing, but this falls into the "needs" category of your budget. Just try to keep your overall rental expenses under 35% of your monthly income.

DOTTiE HERMAN

CEO OF REAL ESTATE FIRM DOUGLAS ELLIMAN

WHICH WORDS DEFINE YOU?

Persistence, ambition, perseverance.

WHAT'S YOUR JOB?

I'm the CEO of real estate firm Douglas Elliman. I set the vision of the company, lead the company, and get everyone involved in the success of the company, regardless of their positions. I love building a winning culture where everyone is included and not competing with one another.

WHAT'S THE CHANGE YOU'RE LOOKING TO CREATE IN THE WORLD?

My goal is to help women overcome obstacles and advance their careers. When women are trying to climb the corporate ladder, they have a lot of things to balance with work, family, and social lives. You can't give 100% to every single thing at all times, and I love helping women find the path that's right for them.

TELL US ABOUT YOUR FIRST JOB.

My first job was at a health spa. I started out teaching an exercise class and eventually moved into sales, helping recruit new members to join the health club. Eventually, I worked my way up to run the spa.

WHAT'S THE BIGGEST MONEY MISTAKE YOU EVER MADE?

I was so involved with building my company that I never concentrated on my personal finances. The truth is, not everyone will enjoy managing their money. If you don't enjoy it, find someone you trust to manage yours for you. It's not how much you make that counts—it's what you save.

WHAT'S THE SMARTEST MONEY MOVE YOU EVER MADE?

I learned early on to always take 10% of whatever I earned and put it aside in savings. At times, it seemed so trivial. Why would I bother even saving just a few dollars? But over time, it really does add up.

TELL US A MONEY STORY THAT MADE YOU WHO YOU ARE TODAY.

I bought my first house before I was ever in real estate. When I was in high school, I collected a small amount of money from a settlement from being in a car crash, and I was planning to use that money to go on a trip, but my father pulled me aside and said, "Nope, buy real estate." All I could afford was this one ugly house. It was so tiny, but it was in a good location. I rented it out, and then I used that money for a down payment on something bigger and better.

WHAT ONE PIECE OF CAREER ADVICE WOULD YOU GIVE TO YOUR YOUNGER SELF?

When you are passionate about something, go after your dreams, and don't surround yourself with people who tell you that you can't.

WHAT ONE PIECE OF MONEY ADVICE WOULD YOU GIVE TO YOUR YOUNGER SELF?

As women, we tend to want to care for everyone else, but we should take care of ourselves first.

WHAT THREE THINGS DOES EVERY TEEN NEED TO KNOW ABOUT REAL ESTATE?

1. Location, location, location. Buy the cheapest thing you can find in the best area.

2. If you don't have the money to buy something yourself, go in with a couple of friends.

3. Find a good real estate mentor who can walk you through your purchase.

TO-DO LIST FOR PART 3: USE IT

Hey hey hey . . . who just completed part 3? Looks like YOU to us. Here are a couple of exercises to help you remember what you learned:

Spending Your Values. One of the ways we can make ourselves happiest about our spending decisions is by being sure they line up with what we really value in life. So you're going to make a list of the last ten to twenty things you bought or spent money on (include services, like manicures, as well as things). Try to think of the big ones and the small ones. Then go back through it and ask yourself these questions: How do I feel about spending that money? Would I do it again?

You may be surprised what this list can teach you about how you want to enjoy your money in the future—and how you may want to avoid spending it. See if you can notice any trends. For example, maybe you get more fulfillment when you buy a present for others. Maybe you usually feel great about items you bought that were more than 50% off. Maybe you always find clothing purchases to be less fulfilling than, say, art supplies or hair dye. Think about this list the next time you go shopping to make sure you're spending your hard-earned dollars in ways that you can feel good about.

Make a list of what you want in your first apartment. Some items on your list will be "must-haves," such as having a bedroom of your own and living in a safe place. Other things will be "nice-to-haves," like having a small outdoor space or access to a community pool. You should also consider things like the length of your commute to work or school (ideally it will be as short as possible, so that you save time + gas money!) and how many roommates you'd like to have. Break out your pen and paper and make two lists, separating items into two categories: Housing Needs and Housing Wants. Then, take your Wants list and rank them in order of importance. When you're on a limited budget, there will be some things you'll need to sacrifice, but you can still find a cute place that you love.

PART 4

GET SCHOOLED

GETTING AN EDUCATION

College Is Only Worth It If You Graduate

Have you ever played the board game Life? There's a point early on where you have two choices: Go to college or get a job. If you choose to go straight to work, you start making money earlier in the game. Going to college takes longer and costs money, but once you're done, you have a shot at higher-paying jobs.

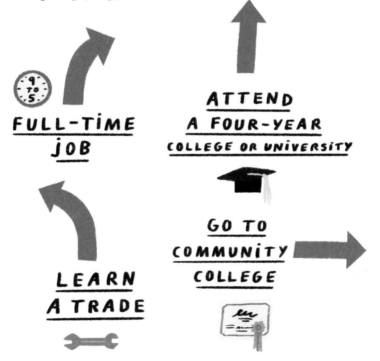

FULL-TIME JOB

ATTEND A FOUR-YEAR COLLEGE OR UNIVERSITY

LEARN A TRADE

GO TO COMMUNITY COLLEGE

That's simplified, of course. In real life, there are other ways to prepare for a good job, including career training programs and apprenticeships. There are also ways to make college less expensive like going to community college and/or applying for financial aid.

But in broad strokes, that's how it works. There's no right answer about which path to choose. The key is to be thoughtful about whatever you do after high school. Here's what you need to know to make the right decision for you—and how to pay for it:

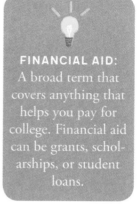

FINANCIAL AID: A broad term that covers anything that helps you pay for college. Financial aid can be grants, scholarships, or student loans.

FOUR-YEAR COLLEGE OR UNIVERSITY

When you close your eyes and picture college, you might imagine a four-year school with a sprawling green quad, old stone buildings, and a good football team. You're picturing a four-year school.

Four-year colleges offer bachelor's degrees and often focus on a liberal arts education—a well-rounded curriculum that sets you up for general success in life but isn't necessarily focused on specific career skills.

Universities, which are usually bigger than colleges, offer bachelor's degrees as well as advanced degrees like master's degrees and doctorates. They tend to have a strong research focus. (A plus if you're interested in a science-related field because you may be able to get research experience.)

Some careers require a bachelor's degree plus an advanced degree like a master's degree or doctorate. To be a doctor, dentist, or lawyer, for instance, you need to go to medical, dental, or law school after earning your undergraduate degree. For a career in academia (to become a college professor, for example), you likely need a PhD. And certain professionals—like school counselors, nurse practitioners, and urban planners—need at least a master's degree.

COMMUNiTY COLLEGE

Community colleges are local public colleges that are sometimes called two-year, junior, or technical colleges. They're generally much cheaper than four-year schools but serve a different purpose, offering two main paths: career training programs and transfer programs.

- **Career Training Programs:** These give you practical training for a specific career such as dental hygiene, early childhood education, or respiratory therapy. They typically provide hands-on learning and lead to a certificate or an associate of applied science (AAS) degree.
- **Transfer Programs:** This is for students who want to get general college classes like English and math out of the way before transferring to a four-year school to earn a bachelor's degree. You can earn an associate's degree at a community college before transferring, which generally takes two years as a full-time student. If you're going this route, meet with your academic advisor regularly to plan out how your credits will transfer.

NON-COLLEGE OPTIONS

College isn't right for everyone, and it's okay if it's not for you. Anna Wintour, editor in chief of *Vogue*; Rachael Ray, Food Network star; and Mary Kay Ash, founder of the Mary Kay cosmetics company, either didn't go to college or didn't finish. There are other ways to train for a career like:

- **Apprenticeships:** How does getting paid to learn skills on the job sound? These are common for trade workers (like carpenters and electricians) and some big companies in fields like business and technology.

- **Bootcamps:** These are short-term, intensive programs that teach coding, data science, and other tech skills. Their goal is to get you career-ready. But they can be expensive, and you won't earn a degree.

- **Military:** You can enlist for active duty right after high school or train to be an officer, which requires a college diploma. The military has many different programs that can help you pay for college either during or after your service.

- **Trade schools:** Sometimes known as vocational or career schools, trade schools offer hands-on training for professions such as cosmetology, medical assisting, and culinary arts. They may lead to an associate's degree or certificate. Do your homework, though. Trade schools—particularly for-profit ones—can be expensive and vary in quality.

- **Work:** By getting a job straight out of high school, you'll start making money ASAP and gain valuable, real-world experience. But without any post-high-school training, you may be limited in the jobs you can get and how much you can earn during your lifetime.

SHOULD YOU TAKE A GAP YEAR?

A gap year is an intentional break between high school and college. It can be a time to travel, intern, volunteer, work, or do a combination of those things. Structured gap year programs range in price from super expensive to very affordable—in some cases you can actually *earn* money.

Taking a gap year can be a way to explore your interests—especially if you're undecided about your college major. It could also enable you to work and save money for college. If you're intrigued, here are a few ideas to help:

- Live and work on an organic farm through the organization Worldwide Opportunities on Organic Farms (WWOOF).
- Stay with a host family while volunteering in a foreign country to immerse yourself in a new language and culture.
- Join AmeriCorps National Civilian Community Corps (NCCC) and do hands-on work around the country to help tackle issues like sustainability, respond to natural disasters, build houses, and more.

But like everything, gap years aren't for everyone. Critics say that you could lose momentum and never end up going to college. Also, a study by the Federal Reserve Bank of New York found that taking a gap year could cost you $90,000 over a lifetime by delaying your entrance into the workforce.

HOW TO CHOOSE A COLLEGE

It's tempting to choose a college based on a gorgeous campus, an impressive name, or a sports team . . . But college can be one of the biggest investments you ever make, so it's a decision worth being extra thoughtful about.

Even with smaller purchases—like going to a restaurant or buying a pair of boots—you might look at multiple options, research them (read reviews, look at ratings, etc.), and compare prices before making a decision.

With college, you essentially want to do the same thing on a much bigger scale. Here's how:

1. CONSIDER MULTIPLE SCHOOLS AND MAJORS

Experts recommend applying to around six to eight schools—including a mix of "safeties" and "reach" colleges. But before you even get to the application stage, you can consider many more than that.

Visit colleges in person if possible. (This is the best way to get a feel for each school's culture and to talk to actual students.) Take an official tour, sure, but also work up the courage to ask random students what they like—and don't like—about the school.

Consider different majors, too. Your field of study and the particular program you choose matter more for lifetime earnings than the level of the degree you earn.

In some cases, certificates and associate's degrees can lead to equal- or higher-paying jobs than bachelor's degrees—but it all depends on what you study. For instance, people with certificates in construction trades have roughly the same median earnings (between $40,001 and $50,000 per year) as people with bachelor's degrees in liberal arts and humanities, according to a Georgetown University report. People with an associate's degree in engineering have higher median earnings between $50,001 and $60,000.

2. RESEARCH YOUR OPTIONS

There's no perfect way to identify the best school for you. However, there are some key statistics that highlight how effective colleges are at preparing students to graduate and get a good job. Look at:

- **Graduation Rate.** Surprisingly, just 60% of students who start a bachelor's program earn a degree within four years. But this varies widely by school. You want to know—what's the *four-year* graduation rate? Every extra semester adds time and money to your college investment.
- **Average Salary after Graduation.** How much money can you reasonably expect to make once you earn a diploma? If possible, zero in on the average earnings among graduates of the degree programs you're considering—this is one of the best ways to estimate the return on your college investment.
- **Typical College Debt.** Even after you graduate and start making money, you'll have to pay back any student debt you have, plus interest. Look at the median total student loan debt among grads of each school and what that looks like in terms of the monthly payments you'll have to make.

You can find a lot of this information through the College Scorecard, a tool developed by the Department of Education. But in some cases, you may need to directly ask a college admissions representative.

3. COMPARE PRICES

It's easy to go online and look up tuition prices and room and board costs. But you want to look at a different number: The cost for students after they cash in any grants and scholarships is

TUITION: The cost of classes or a course of study.

known as the net price. You can't truly know *your* net price until after you apply for admission and financial aid. However, schools are required to have an online calculator to help you estimate— you can find these net price calculators through the Department of Education.

Let's say a college's average yearly cost (including tuition, fees, books and supplies, room and board, and other living expenses) is $60,000. You qualify for a $18,000 academic scholarship and $15,000 in need-based grant money. Your net price is $27,000.

When you look at prices like this, you might find that schools that are seemingly too expensive are actually more affordable than lower-priced colleges. Here are the most recent college cost statistics, according to the College Board:

Average Annual Cost of Attendance for 2020–21: Sticker Price vs. Net Price

	Sticker price (Published price)	Net Price (What students actually pay)
Public two-year college (Community college)	$18,550	$14,560
Public four-year colleges (For in-state students)	$26,820	$19,490
Private four-year colleges	$54,880	$33,220

i↳ COLLEGE WORTH iT? ONLY iF YOU GRADUATE

Even with the steep price tag, college is generally worth it if you limit your student debt and graduate with the degree you want. Statistically, people who graduate college earn more and have lower unemployment rates compared to people who don't.

But college is NOT worth it if you don't graduate. This may seem like a no-brainer (duh, of course you're going to graduate), but far too many students start college then leave before earning their degree.

Not earning a diploma is especially dangerous if you have student debt. You'll still be on the hook for the money you borrowed (plus interest), but without the college degree, it may be difficult to earn enough money to afford the payments.

PAYiNG FOR YOUR DEGREE

Paying for your college degree will probably involve piecing together money from many different sources: savings (from you and maybe your parents), income from jobs, grants, scholarships, and student loans.

Financial aid is a broad term that covers anything that helps you pay for college. Some types of financial aid are better than others—here's what you need to know plus tips for saving money on college overall:

TYPE↳ OF FiNANCiAL AiD

Financial aid ranges from money you don't have to pay back (known as **gift aid**) to money you have to pay back with interest (student loans).

Some aid is based on your financial situation (known as need-based aid), and other aid is based on your abilities (known as merit-based aid). Here are the main types of financial aid listed in order of how you should use them:

1. GRANTS

Grants are money for college that you don't have to pay back. They're almost always need-based, which means you qualify if your family is considered low-income. The largest college grant program is the federal government's Pell Grant program, and there are also grants from state governments.

2. SCHOLARSHIPS

You don't have to pay scholarships back either, which is why they're also up at the top of the list. Scholarships are typically merit-based, so you can get them regardless of your financial need. Some merit scholarships come from the schools themselves and are used to attract top students. They're often based on your GPA and standardized test scores. Then there are scholarships from private organizations, including businesses, professional associations, and community groups. You might be able to secure these scholarships through volunteer work, an essay you write about your community, or even by participating in pageants.

3. STUDENT LOANS

Student loans are borrowed money that you have to pay back with interest. You start making payments six months after you graduate college, and it generally takes anywhere from ten to thirty years to pay them off.

Take a breath; we know it sounds scary. The key with student loans is to borrow wisely—and know what you're getting yourself into. In an ideal world, you don't want to borrow more—in total—than you will earn in your first year out of school. That may mean making sure your college search includes schools that want you (because your GPA is higher than its average GPA, or because you're a great French horn player, and they need one for the marching band).

But understanding student loans is important, too. There are two main types of student loans:

- **Federal Student Loans.** These come from the government and have a variety of names (including direct loans and Stafford loans). They're generally better than private ones because there are programs that can make repayment easier, and they typically have lower interest rates, which means you'll spend less to pay them off over time. Every student qualifies for federal student loans. Certain need-based loans are subsidized, which means they do not accrue (or add) interest while you're enrolled in school or during deferment periods.
- **Private Student Loans.** These are loans you get from banks and other private lenders. Unlike federal loans, which any student can qualify for, you need good credit (or a parent or guardian with good credit to co-sign) to get one. Private loans don't have any of the repayment perks that federal student loans have and typically have higher interest rates, too.

Under these umbrellas of federal and private student loans, there are many more types of loans as well. We've made you a handy chart so you can check them out at a glance:

	Subsidized Federal Loans (Stafford)	Non-Subsidized Federal Loans	Plus Loans	Private Loans
Who borrows the $?	Students	Students	Parents or graduate students	Students and/or parents
How much can you borrow?	$5,500 to $12,500 per year or $31,000 to $57,500 total	$5,500 to $12,500 per year or $31,000 to $57,500 total	Up to the total cost	Varies
Is there a credit check?	No	No	Yes	Yes
Are they based on financial need?	Yes	No	No	No
Who pays the interest?	The government does as long as you're in school at least as a part-time student, during the six-month grace period after graduation, and during deferment.	You	N/A	N/A
Are they eligible for income-based repayment programs?	Yes	Yes	Yes	No
Are they eligible for student loan forgiveness?	Yes	Yes	Yes	No
How long do you have to pay them back?	10–30 years	10–30 years	10–30 years	5–15 years

Let's put this into perspective. Say you major in education and become an elementary school teacher—a profession where the 2019 median pay was $59,420.

If you had roughly the same amount of student debt ($60,000) with 5% interest, you'd owe about $636/month for ten years. Your take-home pay would be around $3,700/month, which would mean about 17% of each paycheck would go toward paying back your student loans.

With that math, you can see why it's so important to avoid borrowing more than you'll be able to afford to repay. If you instead studied computer science to become a software developer—a career where the 2019 median pay was $107,510—you'd be in a very different position. Unfortunately, it's on you to keep the amount you decide to borrow in check—because lenders are all too willing to let you borrow more than that.

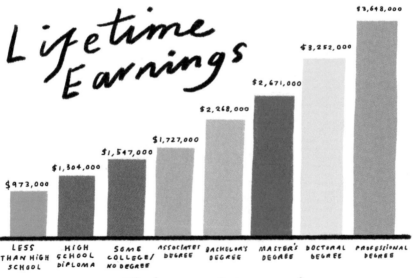

FINANCIAL AID IS A FAMILY AFFAIR

In order to get pretty much any of the financial aid listed above, you need to fill out the FAFSA, which stands for Free Application for Federal Student Aid. It's a form that collects a lot of detailed information about your (and your family's) financial situation in order to determine how much financial aid you need.

Submit the FAFSA before you apply for college, even if you think you won't qualify for need-based aid, because you also need it in order to get federal student loans and many merit-based scholarships.

After filling out the FAFSA, check with the financial aid offices at each college you're applying to and see if they require any additional applications for grants and scholarships. Some schools, particularly elite private ones, require an application called the CSS Profile. Finally, apply to as many outside scholarships as possible.

WAYS TO SAVE MONEY ON COLLEGE

Even with financial aid, college is still expensive. Here are some ways to lower your college costs and limit student loans:

- **Earn College Credits for Less.** The Advanced Placement (AP) program and College Level Examination Program (CLEP) help you earn college credit by taking tests to demonstrate your knowledge. Just remember to make sure your chosen college accepts those credits once it's time to enroll!
- **Go to a Less Expensive College.** This could mean going to a community college then transferring or going to a school that offers you more financial aid. (Remember: Compare costs based on the net price, not the sticker price.)
- **Graduate on Time or Early.** The faster you finish college, the less

you have to pay. Meet with your academic advisor regularly to make sure you're taking the right courses in order to graduate.

- **Get Good Grades and Standardized Test Scores.** The better your GPA and ACT or SAT scores are, the more money in college scholarships you'll likely get. So study!
- **Negotiate for More Financial Aid.** You or a parent can contact a college's financial aid office to appeal your financial aid offer and ask for more. You'll be most successful if you can prove that your family's financial situation has recently changed or if you have a competing offer from a similar type of school.

HOW TO TALK TO YOUR PARENTS ABOUT PAYING FOR COLLEGE

College is an expensive investment, and it's something you'll need to discuss with your parent or guardian if you haven't already. Some families will be able to contribute to your college education, while others won't. If your family is planning to contribute, they will want to talk to you about it, too, and they'll be happy that it's a conversation you want to have!

Pick a time to talk to your parents when you won't be interrupted. It's a great idea to do this during your sophomore or junior year of high school before you start applying to colleges.

Say: "Hey, can we find time to talk about college together?"

GAUGE THEIR WILLINGNESS TO CONTRIBUTE

Get a sense of whether your parents are planning to pay for any part of your college costs. Every family is different, and yours might not be able to contribute. That's okay! It's still important to have the conversation so you can better understand your options.

Say: "I know college is really expensive, and I'm trying to make a plan to pay for it. Are you able to help in any way?"

EXPLAIN THAT YOU NEED THEIR HELP WITH THE FAFSA

In most cases, you'll need to include your parents' tax information and other financial details on the FAFSA regardless of whether they're helping you pay for college.

Say: "I understand if you can't help pay for college, but I need you to please help me complete the FAFSA. Otherwise, I could miss out on a lot of financial aid."

FAFSA: The Free Application for Federal Student Aid. It's a form you have to fill out before you apply to college in order to determine how much financial aid you'll qualify for.

Use this conversation as a jumping-off point. As you explore your next steps toward a successful career (whatever that means for you), don't be afraid to ask questions. Your high school counselors, college advisors, parents, and let's be honest, the internet, are all great resources. Check out StudentAid.gov for more info.

TL;DR

CHAPTER 11 KEY TAKEAWAYS

- Whether or not college is for you, you've got options! You can go to a four-year university, attend a community college, join the military, apply to trade school, take an apprenticeship or bootcamp, or head straight to work. There's no right answer about which path to choose. The key is to be thoughtful about whatever you do after high school—and know how you're going to pay for it.
- Choosing a college can be tough. To make the best choice for you, consider multiple schools and majors, research your options, compare prices (making sure to distinguish between sticker price and net price), and make a college visit whenever you can.
- Student debt can be scary if you get in over your head. Always look to borrow as little as you possibly can—future you will thank you. In general, try not to borrow more than you expect to earn in your first year out of college.
- There are tons of ways to save money on college. You can earn college credits for less with the AP program and CLEP, you can go to a cheaper college, you can graduate on time or early, and you can negotiate for more financial aid.

İLHAN
OMAR

US CONGRESSIONAL REPRESENTATIVE FOR MINNESOTA

WHICH WORDS DEFINE YOU?

Advocate, truth-teller, organizer, passionate, pragmatic, honest.

WHAT'S YOUR JOB?

I'm the congresswoman for Minnesota's Fifth District in the US House of Representatives. As a member of Congress, I get to introduce and advance legislation that improves the lives of people in my district and across our country.

WHAT'S THE CHANGE YOU'RE LOOKING TO CREATE IN THE WORLD?

I'm fighting for an America where everyone can achieve their full potential and live a dignified life. In Congress, I have championed policies that will create a more equitable America where every person is housed, is paid a living wage, is breathing clean air, and is not burdened with student debt.

WHAT WAS YOUR FIRST JOB?

My first job was as a Target cashier in high school, and I made a minimum wage salary of around $7 per hour.

WHAT'S THE BIGGEST MONEY MISTAKE YOU EVER MADE?

The biggest mistake I made was taking out student loans to attend a for-profit college. As a young immigrant and first-generation college student, I did not know at the time how predatory these institutions were.

TELL US A MONEY STORY THAT MADE YOU WHO YOU ARE TODAY.

Find ways to stretch a dime. When I was a college student and raising two young children, I meal prepped every Sunday, cooking stews, grains, and porridges so my kids could have nutritious food prepared. This saved us a lot of time and money.

WHAT ONE PIECE OF CAREER ADVICE WOULD YOU GIVE TO YOUR YOUNGER SELF?

I would tell my younger self to refuse to give oxygen to people who don't have your best interests at heart. Early on in my career, I learned to deal with criticism and people misunderstanding my intentions. Now, as a politician, I'm subjected to constant criticism and critique—but I don't let it control me.

WHAT ONE PIECE OF MONEY ADVICE WOULD YOU GIVE TO YOUR YOUNGER SELF?

Learn how to budget early.

WHAT ARE THE THREE THINGS YOU WISH YOU KNEW ABOUT YOUR COLLEGE EXPERIENCE BEFORE YOU WALKED THROUGH THE DOOR AT FRESHMAN ORIENTATION?

As was typical of many refugees and immigrants, I was ignorant of the vast higher education landscape. I attended a trades program and later transferred to a four-year university. I was a young mother trying to navigate a whole new life. When I entered college, I didn't fully understand the student loan process, the importance of getting enough sleep, and that it was okay to follow your passions and change your college major.

12

YOUR CAREER—AND YOUR PAYCHECK!

Yes, You Should Start Thinking about Your Options Now

Filmmaker Ava DuVernay started her career as a publicist but transitioned into filmmaking with her first movie at age thirty-two. Senator Elizabeth Warren started her career as a teacher, decided to go to law school, and eventually pursued a career in politics.

Why are we telling you this? Because choosing a career is a) tough, and b) something even very famous women change up along the way. That said, giving some thought to what you want to do for work once you're done with school (whatever path you pursue) is a smart thing to do. So let's start here:

YOUR EARNING POTENTIAL

In the last chapter, we talked about your college major and how your field of study is often a pretty good forecaster of the salary you can expect in the future. But let's take a step back to acknowledge "often" isn't "always." HerMoney CEO Jean Chatzky, who majored in English in college, wound up with a lucrative career in finance. How? Her English degree (with a side dish of college theater) made her a pretty great communicator of all things financial.

So although it's important to think about your career in the context of how much your job will pay, you shouldn't choose your college trajectory solely on future earning potential, says Allison Cheston, a career advisor based in New York City. It's much more important—and more interesting!—to select your major and classes based on what you enjoy and what you're curious about. You'll have time during the school year and during summers to find internships and volunteer opportunities that will help shape your career path.

Just try to look for ways to make yourself marketable no matter what you're studying. By adding a double major in physics (or a concentration in marketing as Chatzky did), you can significantly improve your earning potential while doing what you love, Cheston explains.

HOT FIELDS TO CONSIDER

FINTECH

Finance + technology = working for an online bank, a cryptocurrency firm, or a brokerage/investment firm.

Degree suggestions: A bachelor's degree in computer science or mathematics

Average salary: $140,000 per year

AGRITECH

Agriculture + a side of technology = working for vertical farming companies or getting involved with modern greenhouse design.

Degree suggestions: A bachelor's degree in agricultural engineering, civil engineering, or computer science plus a master's degree in a similar field

Average salary: $74,300 per year

ENVIRONMENTAL LAWYER

♥ the environment? Then work to solve issues of land conservation, water quality, and pollution.

Degree suggestions: A bachelor's degree in environmental science plus a law degree (known as a JD or juris doctorate)

Average salary: $113,000 per year

INNOVATION CONSULTING

You (yes, you) can improve how businesses function—helping companies to grow and to better please their customers.

Degree suggestions: Major in English, anthropology, or anything that allows you to perfect your writing and research skills

Average salary: $97,000 per year

ORGANIZATIONAL PSYCHOLOGY

Psychology + business = figuring out new ways to improve working environments, communication, and performance.

Degree suggestions: Psychology, sociology, and political science, but make sure you take some consumer behavior courses

Average salary: $96,000 per year

URBAN PLANNING AND RENEWAL

Get involved in building community structures like  and 🏔 while revitalizing cities and towns.

Degree suggestions: Bachelor's degree in data analytics or instructional design
Average salary: $76,000 per year

SOFTWARE ENGINEER

Who loves gaming? If you do, how about working to create games, software products, and business systems?

Degree suggestions: Coding bootcamp or a bachelor's degree in computer science or computer engineering
Average salary: $105,000 per year

KNOWING YOUR WORTH

Earning money is good. Earning what you're worth is better. But, as we talked about earlier in the book, persistent gender and racial wage gaps make that far from a certainty.

So how can you figure out what you should be paid? And how can you best negotiate and strategize to put that amount in your pocket? Let's take those questions one at a time.

RESEARCH, RESEARCH, AND MORE RESEARCH

There is plenty of salary information publicly available and easily found online at sites like Glassdoor.com and Salary.com. You plug in the job title you're interviewing for and your area of the country, and you'll get a general salary range that will give you an idea of what to ask for when the time comes. The job ads you're answering should also be a source of information. Read enough of them, and you'll start to get a ballpark range of your worth.

And then there's your network. Some people will tell you that you shouldn't talk about how much you make with friends. We disagree! When you learn that a friend with similar skills just landed a job paying, say, $25 an hour or $50,000 a year, it gives you a sense of what to look for. When you share what you're earning in your first job with a friend who is just starting to look, it helps her! Salary transparency is the way of the future—and a huge benefit of closing the wage gap overall. Talk to your friends, girlfriends, boyfriends, classmates—everyone! By helping each other in this way, we can close one small gap at a time.

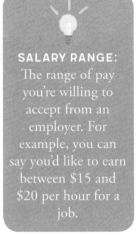

SALARY RANGE: The range of pay you're willing to accept from an employer. For example, you can say you'd like to earn between $15 and $20 per hour for a job.

NEGOTiATiNG YOUR FiRST SALARY

A conversation about pay will happen every time you get hired. If you're coming out of another job, you should know that (in many states) it's illegal for employers to ask what you were previously making. That means you don't have to feel constrained by that number.

negotiation

AGREEMENT

COMMUNICATION

SKILLS

TACTIC

CONTRACT

COLLABORATION

GOAL

If possible, try to get the employer to name their salary first. You can ask something like, "What does this position pay?" or "What is the salary budgeted for this position?" If you can avoid being the first to name a number, you may be better off because the employer may be offering more than you thought, and you could lowball yourself. Once they put out a number—ask for more. Always. Say, "I was hoping for more like . . ." and then name a number that is at least 10% higher, maybe a little more if your research has shown their number is unrealistically low.

Unfortunately, there will be times when you have to answer the question first. That means being ready with a salary range when they ask you the question, "What are you looking to make?" or "What salary range are you looking for?"

Consider your market research, your personal accomplishments and skills, and what you need to earn to live in your town or city. Then aim high—but not too high. Give a number in the middle-top of the range that you discovered in your research.

So, for example, if you found that the starting salary range for a position that you wanted was $35,000 to $40,000, you could start by saying, "I'm looking to make $40,000 to $50,000, but I'm interested in this position and open to negotiating." This lets them know you've done your research, and you value your skills enough to know that you expect to be paid market value—but that you're also excited about the job and willing to meet them in the middle. And remember, there are things other than salary you should be considering here. The amount your company is kicking into the retirement plan and to pay for healthcare count toward your total compensation, too.

Employers want to hire people who know how to advocate for themselves, and they understand that quality spills over into how they behave on the job. So *always* negotiate, even if you think the answer will be "no." It truly never hurts to ask.

WHY THAT VERY FIRST SALARY IS SO IMPORTANT

Here's a depressing statistic. More than half of men negotiate for their first job out of college. Just 7% of women do. That's a problem because every salary impacts the one that comes next. Take a look at how your starting salary impacts your earnings over time.

Let's say your starting salary at your new job is $50,000. At the end of the year, you get a 4% raise, which bumps you up to $52,000. (Most employers will give a raise that is based on a percentage of your old salary rather than just handing you, say, $5,000 as your raise.)

But let's say you negotiated for a higher starting salary of $55,000. That same 4% raise would bump you up to $57,200.

Let's assume you get 4% raises every year for five years in a row:

STARTING SALARY OF $50,000 WITH 4% RAISE EVERY YEAR:

After one year: $52,000
After two years: $54,080
After three years: $56,243.20
After four years: $58,492.93
After five years: $60,832.65

STARTING SALARY OF $55,000 WITH 4% RAISE EVERY YEAR:

After one year: $57,200
After two years: $59,488
After three years: $61,867.52

After four years: $64,342.22
After five years: $66,915.91

You can see how that higher starting salary can make a big difference in your life in a very short time, so never be afraid to ask for more money up front. In fact, asking for more than the initial salary offer you're given should be your default move—hiring managers are impressed by people who know their worth. And, as we've said before, it never (ever!) hurts to ask.

TL;DR

CHAPTER 12 KEY TAKEAWAYS

- What you study in college—and how much you spend and borrow to get your degree—all plays into your future financial equation. While it's important to be thoughtful about what you want to do, you'll probably have several different phases of your career, and it's okay to change your mind! Often, we figure out what we want most in life by eliminating what we don't want.
- Always negotiate. There may be wiggle room for an employer to pay you more, but you'll never find out if you don't ask. If you're not sure what to ask for, there is plenty of salary information publicly available on sites like Glassdoor.com and Salary.com. Pro tip: Whenever you go into a salary negotiation, try to get the employer to name their salary offer first.

DORiANNE
ST FLEUR

FOUNDER AND CEO OF YOUR CAREER GIRL

WHICH WORDS DEFINE YOU?

Leader, decisive, doer.

WHAT'S YOUR JOB?

I'm a performance coach who helps ambitious women of color get clear on their possibilities so they can become corporate powerhouses. I'm also a workplace inclusion strategist. I study, specifically, corporate work culture and how it affects and impacts Black women and other people of color.

WHAT'S THE CHANGE YOU'RE LOOKING TO CREATE IN THE WORLD?

I want to help women of color break generational curses.

TELL US ABOUT YOUR FIRST JOB.

My first real job was as a trade support analyst at an investment bank in New York City. I started straight out of college, and my salary was $50,000 a year. I remember feeling like I'd won the lottery. It took me about five years before I ever even thought about negotiating my salary.

WHAT'S THE BIGGEST MONEY MISTAKE YOU EVER MADE?

Taking out loans to finance a graduate school degree I ended up never finishing. I racked up almost $90,000 in debt. I'm almost brought to tears when I think about what I could've used that money for instead.

WHAT'S THE SMARTEST MONEY MOVE YOU EVER MADE?

Paying off all of my debt. When you don't have debt, you'll be amazed at the reduction in stress and worry in your life.

WHAT'S THE MONEY SECRET YOU ARE KEEPING?

One of my biggest money hurdles I've overcome was getting out of credit card debt. Once I finally did, I vowed that I would never get back in it again. While I do have one credit card that I keep for emergencies, I typically only use cash/debit cards for my purchases, including vacations and other big purchases. If it's not in my budget, I don't buy it.

WHAT ONE PIECE OF CAREER ADVICE WOULD YOU GIVE TO YOUR YOUNGER SELF?

Negotiate your salary. Every single time. Yes, even your first job out of college. Will you get what you want every time? No. But the muscle you're building when it comes to standing your ground and asking for what you want will serve you well.

WHAT ARE YOUR TOP THREE TIPS FOR HAVING THE BEST JOB INTERVIEW EVER?

Understand the real purpose of the interview, which is to show why you're the best candidate for the role. This is your opportunity to demonstrate your experience, so get clear on your V.I.P. (value, impact, and power), and use every question you're asked in your interview.

Value: Specific contributions you have made in past roles.

Impact: How your contributions have contributed to the bottom line of your team and company.

Power: The confidence you have in your ability to get good results in a new role.

The interview isn't about robotically answering questions. It's about building relationships. Take the time to find connection and common ground with your interviewers.

TO-DO LIST FOR PART 4

In this part of the book, we asked you to look out into the near future (college!) and down the road after that (jobs!). Here are a couple of exercises to help crystalize your thoughts on what you just read:

Community College vs. Four-Year University: Talk It Out. Where are your friends planning to go to school after high school? Are they going to get their start at a community college or head straight for a four-year university? See what their plans are and ask them why they made their decision.

What Do You Want to Be When You Grow Up? It's a question we're asked so many times when we're little, and the younger we are, the easier it is to be confident in the answer. But as we get older and we're faced with real decisions about where to go to school, what to major in, where to live, and which career to pursue, things seem a little more . . . murky. The truth is, there are probably several things you could do in life that would make you happy and enable to you earn a good living. Now's the time to make a list. What are five things you enjoy doing, and what could you major in that would let you pursue those passions?

1.
2.
3.
4.
5.

PART 5

LOOK TO THE FUTURE

13

HEALTH is WEALTH

Why Staying Healthy Is a Good Move for Your Life (and a Smart Money Move, Too!)

Your health is everything, regardless of how much money you have and what's going on in your day-to-day life. Good health allows you the freedom to live the life you choose. Over the course of your lifetime, staying healthy can result in BIG money saved because getting sick can mean expensive doctor and hospital visits as well as time off of work.

Unfortunately, none of us can control all aspects of our health. Some health conditions are genetic or inherited. But smart choices now can also impact how healthy you are later and help you save a lot of money on health care costs down the road.

HOW To PROTECT YOUR HEALTH

Eating right and exercising regularly are healthy habits that can be as good for your bank account as they are for your body. Regular physical activity can help prevent type 2 diabetes, heart disease, many types of cancer, depression, and anxiety, according to the CDC. So get up and *move*!

Don't think of exercise strictly as disease prevention—and don't view it as punishment for indulging in your favorite foods, either. Instead, consider exercise one of the keys to living your best life. "Regular movement is your wellbeing bank account that delivers massive returns for your whole life," says Tara Stiles, a global yoga, movement, and wellness expert and the founder of Stråla Yoga. The same goes for eating well. "Your energy levels, overall mood, creativity, productivity, sound sleep, and intuition rely on [having] a healthy body."

How is this in any way about your money? Only in every way. Let's flash forward to future you. If you've stayed healthy, you've got a lot more cash in the bank to fund all the activities that you have the energy to take on.

HEALTHY HABITS THAT CAN SAVE YOU MONEY

Think it's impossible to eat well and stay fit when you're short on time or low on cash? Think again. Here are seven healthy hacks that aren't just cheap—they'll save you money:

- **Eat More Veggies.** This move is good for your heart and your wallet. Plant-based proteins offer more health benefits than meat and tend to be less expensive.
- **Move Your Body.** Head to the gym, pick up your home workout equipment, or walk and bike whenever and wherever it's safe to do so. You'll save on gas costs and add more physical activity to your day—a win-win!
- **Start a Food and Fitness Diary.** Write down what you

eat and how it makes you feel . . .
You'll soon realize that things like
fruits and veggies make you feel a
lot better than fast food or pro-
cessed foods.

- **Say No to Tobacco.** The CDC reports that cigarette
  smoking is responsible for more than 480,000 deaths
  per year in the United States, and according to the
  National Cancer Institute, a pack a day will set you
  back $2,292 per year.

- **Brown Bag Your Lunch.** It's
  cheaper and healthier to pack your
  own. Enough said.
- **Cook!** It's not only cheaper
  than eating out, it's also healthier.
  Plus: leftovers!

- **Drink More Water.** When you choose water over
  soda, you'll save money and calories. And being well-
  hydrated is always a good thing!
- **Get Your Beauty Sleep.** Getting enough sleep makes
  everything better—it even helps with productivity and
  concentration, too.

BAD FOR YOUR HEALTH: DEBT AND THE STRESS IT BRINGS

Just as your health can affect your cash flow, money matters can
impact your health. When you have unanswered questions about your
finances, it's easy to get stressed out. But when you're armed with financial knowledge and an understanding of your personal money picture,
you'll feel in control of your finances and in control of your life.

We also know that there's one big thing that brings on a lot of financial stress: debt. That's why we've put such a big emphasis on making sure that a) when you decide to take on debt, whether it's credit card debt or student loan debt, you do it wisely and with a plan for paying it back, and b) you don't take on more than you need—ever.

There are also three things that are proven to reduce financial stress, according to research from Fidelity. You may not be at the point where you can do all these things yet, but put them on your list for the years to come.

1. Be a consistent saver (saving 15% is key but start wherever you can).
2. Have a plan (e.g., those goals we talked about).
3. Create a fund for emergencies.

EVERYTHING YOU NEED TO KNOW ABOUT HEALTH INSURANCE

Even if you're doing all you can to stay healthy, you still need health insurance because illness and accidents happen to everyone at some point, no matter how careful we are.

But what is health insurance, exactly? Think of it like your just-in-case fund. All insurance is like that, really. Auto insurance is just in case you get in a fender bender. Home insurance is just in case of a fire or flood. Health insurance is just in case

you get sick or injured. When you have health insurance and you need to go see a doctor or take a trip to the emergency room, your insurance policy kicks in and helps you pay for your medical bills.

But let's back up and talk about insurance for a sec. We talked about this term in chapter 10 with auto insurance and renter's insurance. But there are lots of different types of insurance—you can purchase insurance to cover everything from jewelry to body parts (we've heard of some celebs insuring certain, ahem, *ass*ets). In its simplest terms, insurance provides financial protection for something that would otherwise be very, *very* expensive to replace or repair (like, say, your health or your grandmother's heirloom necklace). It's a way to prepare for the worst-case scenario—even if you hope the worst never happens, it's always worth being prepared. When you buy an insurance policy, you agree to pay a monthly or annual fee, called a premium, to a company that provides this kind of protection. If and when the worst happens, the company then helps you pay for the cost (e.g., ACL surgery or replacing the vintage clasp on that necklace). Here are some essential terms to understanding a few more insurance basics:

Deductible: As we mentioned in chapter 10, a deductible is the amount you're responsible for paying *before* your insurance kicks in. This is an out-of-pocket expense that you're responsible for paying on top of your insurance premium. Let's say your deductible is $500 per year. You're responsible for paying $500 (in addition to your premium) before your insurance will start shelling out any dough.

Co-insurance: This refers to the shared cost that you agree to with an insurance company to cover costs beyond your deductible. In essence, once your deductible is met, your insurance company then will cover a certain amount of any charges on your behalf. This is usually expressed as a split (e.g., 80/20, where the insurance covers 80% of any charges and you pay the remaining 20%). Let's say you've paid that $500 deductible and then receive a doctor's bill for $100. Your insurance company will pay $80, and you'll pay the remaining $20.

Co-pay: Depending on your insurance plan, this is often a fixed amount that you'll be required to pay for things like doctor's visits or prescriptions. These are different for each plan, and it's always important to read up on what these charges will be so you're not hit with any surprises. These fees are often listed on your insurance card. For example, some insurance companies require to you pay $200 if you have to go to the ER. (Super unfair, but that's how it works!)

Buying health insurance can feel like a big step in your adulting journey, but don't let the term scare you—health insurance isn't there just for when you're sick. It helps you pay for regular checkups that could keep you from getting sick in the first place as well as appointments with your dentist and examinations by your gynecologist. If you need to see a therapist, insurance can help pay for that, too.

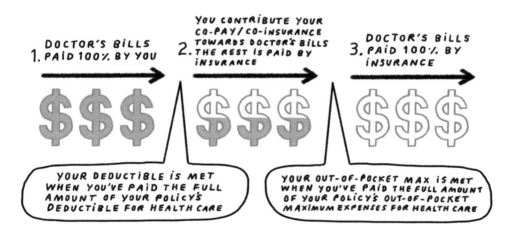

GETTING COVERED

Right now, you may be covered under your parents' health insurance, but it's important that you talk to your parents to see what their plans are for covering you in the years after high school or college. Whatever you decide, in the next few years, you'll need to sign up for a health care plan via the Health Insurance Marketplace, through your university, or through an employer if you're working full time.

If you're going to college, check with your school to find out if there's a health insurance plan specifically for students. These plans are often super affordable but may only cover specific doctors or services, so make sure you read the fine print before you see a doctor. If you are on a parent's plan, you may need to let your school know that you don't need theirs—in some cases, they will charge you for the school plan if they're not notified.

Once you're out of school, there are three basic ways to get health insurance:

AFFORDABLE CARE ACT: A US law passed in 2010 designed to expand access to health insurance. Also called Obamacare.

1. **Stay on a Parent's Plan.** Under the Affordable Care Act, you're allowed to remain on a parent's plan until you hit age twenty-six. In that case, you don't have to take the employer's plan. Staying covered by Mom or Dad is often the best (and cheapest) option.

2. **Get It from an Employer.** If you're working full time (sometimes even part time), you may be eligible to get your health insurance through your employer. This is what most Americans do.

3. **Buy It Yourself.** You can purchase insurance at Healthcare.gov, the marketplace set up under the Affordable Care Act, or from a private marketplace like eHealthInsurance.com.

The one thing you don't want to do? Go without health insurance. Why? Emergencies happen all the time—even to people in their teens and twenties. And trust us, the bills get expensive fast. That's not a chance you want to take.

TL;DR

CHAPTER 13 KEY TAKEAWAYS

- Your health is everything. When you're healthy, you'll be happier overall. Smart choices now can impact how healthy you are later on in life and help you save money on health care expenses.
- You can be healthy whether you're short on time, low on cash, or both. There are free exercise classes happening all the time at your local gym, school, place of worship, or community center, and we can save so much money (and reduce our fat and calorie intakes!) when we eat at home.
- Debt is a stress inducer, and it can lead to serious health problems, including heart disease and depression. That's why it's so important to be smart about the debt you take on in your life.
- You gotta have health insurance, no exceptions. You're likely on your parents' plan now, but eventually you can also get it from your employer or buy it on a health insurance exchange.

JAZZ JENNINGS

TRANSGENDER ADVOCATE, AUTHOR, AND PHILANTHROPIST

WHICH WORDS DEFINE YOU?

Creative, spontaneous, loving, illustrious, courageous.

WHAT'S YOUR JOB?

I'm a cast member in the TV docu-series *I Am Jazz*, which chronicles my life as a transgender girl and how my family and I navigate the world. I'm also a social media influencer and author of two books, *I Am Jazz* and *Being Jazz—My Life as a Transgender Teenager*.

WHAT'S THE CHANGE YOU'RE LOOKING TO CREATE IN THE WORLD?

To reassure transgender youth and their families that it's okay to be different. Life is about accepting who you are, loving yourself, and embracing your uniqueness. Looking back at my life, I'm proud of what I've been able to manifest with the help of my family. It is important that we are conscious observers of our own thoughts and choose to focus on ideas that bring about positive emotions. We all have the ability to choose what we want to think about.

WHAT'S THE BIGGEST MONEY MISTAKE YOU EVER MADE?

When I was twelve, I started a mermaid tail business. I began making mermaid tails and started selling them. However, the materials I needed to make the tails were too expensive, the tails took much longer to make than I thought, and I couldn't keep up with the amount of orders. I ended up having to refund customers and cancel orders. It was a mess.

WHAT'S THE SMARTEST MONEY MOVE YOU EVER MADE?

Joining my family as we founded the TransKids Purple Rainbow. We help kids and families that are struggling. We raise money to help support other organizations like those that offer camps and retreats to trans kids and help homeless transgender youth.

TELL US A MONEY STORY THAT MADE YOU WHO YOU ARE TODAY.

I'm not a frivolous spender. I like to save and don't need more than the basics in life. I'd rather go out to dinner and enjoy good times with family and friends than buy a new pair of shoes or a designer bag.

WHAT'S THE BEST PIECE OF CAREER ADVICE YOU EVER GOT?

To always remember to keep a piece of myself . . . for myself. I enjoy helping others, but I can sometimes be overwhelmed. I need to make sure to practice self-care and stay mentally grounded so I can be a better version of myself, which ultimately helps others.

WHAT ARE THREE EASY WAYS THAT TEENS CAN SAVE MONEY AND BE HEALTHY AT THE SAME TIME?

1. Remember to spend money on items that can serve you better in the future. For instance, save money for a car (which can stay with you into adulthood) instead of buying video games.

2. Make wiser choices when buying food. Steer away from fast food and learn how to make healthy foods at home. It's cheaper and better for your mind and body.

3. Pamper yourself sometimes, but find fun and cheap ways to do so. For instance, host a spa day at home with friends as opposed to spending big bucks at salons.

$$\rule{4cm}{0.4pt} \quad 14 \quad \rule{2cm}{0.4pt}$$

HOW TO MONEY—HAPPILY

Now You Know All the Secrets

At some point in your life (we're guessing here, but we're pretty good at that) someone (Mom? Grandma?) has probably said to you: Money can't buy happiness.

They're kind of wrong about that, and there's plenty of science to back it up. Researchers studying the money/happiness connection have found that money *can* buy happiness, but only to a point. Think about it this way: If you are struggling financially, does another $1, $10, $100, or $1,000 make you happier? You bet it does. Because it pays the rent, puts gas in the car, and puts food on the table. It means that you can stop stressing out and worrying, if only for a little while.

Until you've achieved a comfortable life—and we define that as having a nice place to live, a safe and reliable car or other form of transportation to get you where you need to go, money for groceries and utilities, and the ability to go out and enjoy yourself occasionally, maybe even go on vacation—more money absolutely will kick up your happiness a notch or two. This comfortable life is not a bougie life; it's not a Kardashian life. It's just nice. Once you're there, however, more money won't buy you lasting happiness. (Score one for Mom.)

iT'S ALL iN THE ADAPTATiON

We know what you're thinking. You're thinking: *This is* wrong. *If I had more money, of course I would be happier.* But the secret is in that word "lasting." Lasting means for a long time. It may even mean forever. And here's where the researchers know something you don't.

Once you enter adult life, you'll probably get a job. If this job is like many, every year (or so) you'll get a raise. Woot! Cue the celebration! Time to make some dinner reservations or buy those boots you've looked at online so many times they're now a constant presence in your news feed.

And that's the problem. Human beings are very adaptable creatures. One of the things we adapt to, very quickly, is the amount of money that shows up in our paychecks. We are thrilled the first couple of weeks under that new salary, but then we allow ourselves one extra spin class a week, or we go for the gel manicure rather than the regular one, or we add a streaming subscription (or two). All of a sudden, we can no longer imagine how we ever lived on less. (This is why it's so important that, when you actually get a raise, you increase the amount you're automatically putting in savings pronto!) And those extras—manicures, subscriptions, whatever—that seemed special at first no longer light you up. Your level of happiness is right back where it was.

USE MONEY TO MAKE YOU HAPPY

Let's remind ourselves about one of the basic truths about money. It's a limited resource. And so it makes sense to try to use it in a way that brings us the biggest boost of happiness. Lucky for us, we know (again, research) that there are a bunch of specific ways to do that.

- **Figure Out What You Value and Put Your Money There.** We touched on this earlier, but it's important to remember that one of the things that makes each of us individuals is what we value—what we believe is important (or unimportant) and what we take pleasure in (or dislike). Some people value having exciting new experiences, others value creating cozy spaces where we feel at home, still others value saving money because they want to have enough so they don't have to worry. If you know what you value, then you have a guide for how to use your money to make you happy.

- **Give Experiences a Try.** Although not all people value the same things, there's a lot of evidence that, on average, we get more enjoyment out of experiences than we do out of things. That makes sense, right? When you buy a thing—a new laptop, a sweater, whatever—it's fabulous until all of a sudden the newness wears off. And you catch yourself wanting another new thing. Experiences are different. We post about them on social media, talk about them with our friends, sometimes we even embellish, and when we do this, we get to enjoy them all over again. P.S., There are some things that we buy that we also experience. For example, if you buy a beautiful piece of art and you get a little jolt of pleasure every time you look at it, you're experiencing that thing. That's a pretty good way to use your money, too.

- **Include Other People and/or Causes.** When you spend your money in a way that helps you strengthen your relationships with friends and family, you tend to enjoy these things more. We are happier, overall, when we have stronger emotional ties. So whether you're spending your money on an activity or experience that you enjoy with others or you're spending it doing something for them (picking out the perfect gift), you're headed in the right direction. Or you may just want to consider being generous. More money may not make us more happy, but more giving absolutely does.

REDUCE YOUR MONEY STRESS

How many times in this book have we mentioned that money can stress people out? A lot. We acknowledge that. But there are things you can do that will bring your stress levels down. We clued into this years ago when HerMoney founder Jean Chatzky conducted a study of five thousand people on money and happiness. What she found was that being happy financially was much more about feeling *in control* of your money than the amount of money you have. Here's how to get that control:

- **Set Some Goals.** Goals, simply put, are things you want. What makes them different from things you put on a wishlist is that they are specific, and they have a deadline for when you want to have them. People who have goals are happier than people who don't because they aren't just wandering aimlessly in one direction or

another—they're moving with purpose toward something they have decided they want. You know all about goals because we talked about them on page 61. So set some.

- **Save Something (Then Visit Your Savings).** Jean's research found that when people were consistently saving 5% of what they were earning, they were happier. Now, as we've talked about earlier in the book, that's not enough to build a future on—we want you saving more like 15%—but it's the habit of saving that's really important. Then sign into your account regularly and watch your money add up. (That's the fun part!)

- **Don't Procrastinate.** Have you ever noticed how your parents handle the bills? Do they put them off for a while or pay them ASAP? If they do the latter, they're happier. Why? Because they don't have to worry that a bill is going to be late or slip through the cracks. When it comes to everything in your financial life, the less you put off doing things, the happier you'll be. Procrastinating (as you know if you've ever put off having an uncomfortable conversation) wakes you up in the middle of the night and occupies your mind when you're trying to study for a test or do something else important. Let's not.

Groceries

- **Document Your Gratitude.** Good things happen in all of our lives every day. Sometimes we get too stressed out to notice them. This is why keeping a gratitude journal can be a helpful stress reducer. And it's simple to do. Just put a notepad on your nightstand. Every night before you go to sleep, jot down three things that you're grateful for from that day. Try to get specific about it. "I am grateful for the hour I spent snuggling with my cat." "I am grateful that I finally understood the geometry lesson." "I am grateful that tonight is daylight savings and I get an extra hour of sleep." Then go back and read over your prior entries every once in a while. You'll start to see that there is a pattern of good things in your life and that will make you happier, too.

USE YOUR MONEY (AND YOUR TIME) TO BUILD THE WORLD YOU BELIEVE IN

If there's a theme that has run through this chapter, it's that giving = happiness. But you want to give wisely. There are millions, literally millions, of charitable organizations that would like you to choose them. So how do you decide among them?

- **Figure Out What You Believe In.** When it's your money, where to give it away is a personal choice just like where to spend it is. There are some charities that will weigh on your heart more than others. Perhaps someone in your life had (or has) a terrible disease, and above all else, you want to see that disease cured. Perhaps you can't stand it when you hear about animals in shelters waiting to get adopted (and it's just not possible to adopt them all yourself). Knowing what matters to you is the very first step to focusing your giving.

- **Choose Your Community or the World.** Once you've got an issue or cause that resonates, it can be helpful to decide if you want to try to support it on a local, national, or even global level. The benefit to going local is that you may be able to get involved by volunteering in person or by attending nearby events.

- **Check Them Out.** In the world of charities, sadly, there are scams and rip-offs. Before you give money to any organization, you want to check them out by making sure they're an official charity or 501(c)(3). Then head to CharityNavigator.org or GuideStar.org to find out what a charity's rating is and where they're really spending the dollars you donate.

- **No money? No problem.** About one-quarter of people in America volunteer. They give their time to organizations they care about and that has huge value (plus it can be social and being with other people generally gives us a nice boost in happiness). An organization called VolunteerMatch.com can help you find opportunities. Go to their website and type in your location, when you'd like to volunteer, and they'll match you up. Folks in your school's guidance office may be able to help as well.

CHAPTER 14 KEY TAKEAWAYS

- While it's true that money can't buy happiness, it *can* make life easier. When you have enough money to pay your bills, save for a rainy day, and take a vacation, you have *enough*—and having enough and being comfortable is what we want to work toward in our financial lives.
- There are several ways we can use our money to improve the quality of our lives and the lives of others. One way is to figure out what you value and put your money there. You can figure this out by tracking your spending and seeing which items you bought make you feel *good*.

- Reducing money stress is another big way that we can improve our lives. We do this by setting goals, saving at least 5% of what we earn, not procrastinating big financial decisions (or even little ones like paying bills), and by documenting our gratitude.

- Whenever you start to make more money, make sure you put a portion of your new salary into savings *immediately*; otherwise it's very easy to spend what you make without ever increasing your contribution into savings.

TO-DO LiST FOR PART 5:

Take a deep breath with us. In. Out.

You've made it to the end of this book. You've learned and done it ALL. And we are proud of you. More importantly, we want YOU to be proud of you! Allow yourself to feel it! Here are a few more exercises to wrap up your journey:

Healthy Habits Now. We know that eating right and exercising regularly are two of the most important healthy habits we can develop. What are your favorites in each category? Make a list of your favorite healthy foods like salads, baked potatoes, grilled chicken, or broccoli. Then make a list of your favorite exercises like soccer practice, yoga class, or running. Now think about some opportunities you might have to interject more of these healthy habits into your life. For example, are there more chances in your week to grab a salad instead of a burger? On the morning when your first class starts later in the day, could you get up and go for a run? Find ways to get more of those healthy habits in whenever you can!

Start a Gratitude Journal. Grab a notebook and a pen and put it on your bedside table. Each night before you go to sleep, start jotting down three good things that happened that day. Three things you're grateful for. They can be small things or big ones. Consistency is key. Then each week, retrace your steps and read your whole list. What you'll see is that there are always things to be thankful for!

Insta-Spend. We know that money is a limited resource. After you track your spending to see how each item (or experience) makes you feel, add this question to the exercise: Have you ever bought something you saw advertised on social media or something worn or used by an influencer? What did you think of that product? Did it inspire you to buy again or to save your money next time? What have you learned from your social media buying experience(s)?

Don't Worry, Be Happy . . . We know that giving back makes us happy. You may not have money to be philanthropic right now, but one day you will, and you can always give your time as a volunteer. What are some causes that you want to support? Have you ever given your money or time before? How did it make you feel?

YOUR NEXT BIG STEPS

Woot! You've just taken some incredibly important steps to educate and empower yourself as you spread your financial wings, and all of us at Her-Money think that's a-may-zing.

We hope the words and examples found in this book have helped set you up for success, but we also know that, throughout your life, there will be many money frustrations, money mistakes, and money regrets. That's just the way life works. But in every one of those is a lesson that you'll never forget—a lesson that will make you a better investor, a better negotiator, a smarter spender, and a better advocate—for yourself and others.

Remember that you don't have to be passionate about money to be good with *your* money. And you don't have to love budgeting in order to make a budget that will keep your financial life humming along completely stress-free. In other words, you don't have to pursue personal finance for a living like Jean and Kathryn, but you *do* have a responsibility to get the women in your life talking about their money. Why? Because when your friends, sisters, cousins, roommates—every woman you know—gets more engaged with her finances, the more empowered *all* women become. And if we're going to close the gender pay gap, it's going to take all of us uplifting one another and advocating for one another whenever we need help.

When you're done with this book, pass it on to someone else who you think might enjoy it. And if you learn something new you'd like us to know or have a question about something we didn't cover, you can always email us at MailBag@HerMoney.com, and we'll get right back to you.

Remember that you are shaping your own financial destiny every day with every choice you make. We want the adventure that's coming up for you—aka life—to be just that: an adventure and not a grind. If you follow the steps we laid out, there's more fun in store for you than you can imagine. We hope you're inspired to take the next steps on your financial journey with confidence and to earn, save, invest, donate, and go on to find success in all the ways you most desire.

We know you can do it. Because YOU can do anything.

ACKNOWLEDGMENTS

Every book is a team effort—this one more than most—and we want to use this space not only to shower the reporters and writers who dug into these chapters with love, but also to give a shout out to the sources who so graciously gave us their time and information. So . . . with that in mind.

The byline says "the HerMoney team." Who is that, exactly?

Rebecca Cohen adroitly helmed the sections on earning money and starting your own business.

Teddy Nykiel deftly navigated the chapter on paying for college and the myriad ways our futures can take shape.

Javacia Harris Bowser brought her keen eye and life experience to the topic of homeownership and racial inequities, and educated us all on healthy habits that can make our lives better.

Dayana Yochim tackled the topic of saving and investing with her trademark warmth, wisdom, and humor.

Jessica Patel helped us all chart a course through securing our first car and apartment.

Molly Povich and Hayden Field—Well, they have fingerprints all over the manuscript in scattered bursts.

We are so grateful to them all for pouring themselves into this project.

This book was shepherded to publication under the fine and watchful eye of Kate Meltzer, our editor at Macmillan, and her amazing team—Aurora Parlagreco, Starr Baer, Kathy Wielgosz, Allene Cassagnol, Jennifer Healey, Molly Ellis, Kelsey Marrujo, and Emilia Sowersby. Thank you, Kate!

Heather Jackson is—and we say this in an absolutely unbiased way—just the best agent on the planet. You would be lucky to have her in your corner. We know we are. xo.

We fell in love with illustrator Nina Cosford on Instagram and were so jazzed to get the word that she was willing to collaborate with us on this project. Our new aim in life: to perfect our own messy buns à la Nina.

When you are a financial reporter—any reporter for that matter, but a financial reporter in particular—good sources are those people you go back to again and again because a) they know their stuff, and b) they can explain it clearly. We are in debt to:

Allison Cheston, Career Development Expert

Karen Ortiz, Administrative Judge at the EEOC

Beverly Harzog, credit card expert and consumer finance analyst

Julie Sherrier, Senior Managing Editor at Lending Tree

Matt Schulz, Chief Credit Analyst at Lending Tree

Trae Bodge, Smart Shopping Expert

Ariel Lopez, CEO of Knack

Diane Mulcahy, Author of *The Gig Economy*

Katica Roy, Founder and CEO of Pipeline

Jeanette Thornton, Senior Vice President of Product, Employer, and Commercial Policy at America's Health Insurance Plans

Tara Stiles, founder of Stråla Yoga

Anthony ONeal, personal finance expert with Ramsey Solutions

John Girouard, President and CEO of Capital Asset Management Group

There are some people who keep HerMoney going, and it feels appropriate to thank them here. So, a big hug to Gary Greenwald, Charles DeMontebello, Tucker Dalton, Niki Offutt, Rebecca Jones, Lindsay Tigar, Casandra Andrews, Zoe Fisher, as well as our sponsors and partners. We so appreciate you!

Finally, to our families and loved ones. On Kathryn's side: Ben, Rod and Jo Ellen, Dee, Sydney, Ashley, Julia, Ben, Will, Chelsea, and Tila. Yakoke. You inspire me every day. On Jean's side: Eliot, Jake, Julia, Sam and Shelby, Emily, Elaine and Bob, Dave, Ali, and Eric. I love you all.

xox,

Kathryn and Jean

GLOSSARY

401(k): A work-based retirement account, sponsored by an employer, that lets you make pre-tax contributions directly from your paycheck. Similar accounts include 403(b)s and 457s.

Affordable Care Act: A US law passed in 2010 designed to expand access to health insurance. Also called Obamacare.

Allowance: An amount of money you receive, often from parents, at regular intervals. Sometimes you work for an allowance, sometimes you don't.

Annual fee: A yearly charge for carrying a particular credit card.

Apprenticeship: Learning a skill, art, or trade by working side-by-side with someone who does it.

APR (Annual Percentage Rate): The cost of borrowing or the amount you're paid for saving, in percentage terms, including your interest rate and any additional fees.

Asset: Something valuable that you own. Cash, homes, cars, art, and jewelry are assets. In the context of investing, people refer to the money in their investment portfolio as assets.

ATM: Automatic Teller Machines. Transaction portals that allow you to withdraw money, deposit money, check your balances, and perform other bank activities.

Authorized user: A person granted permission to use another person's credit card. They typically receive a card in their own name and may have a separate credit limit, but are not ultimately responsible for paying the bill.

Automate: When you use technology to accomplish a task you would otherwise do by hand. Saving, investing, and bill-paying can all be automated so you don't have to think about it.

Balance: The amount of money you have in a bank or brokerage account at a particular time or the amount you have due on an account, like a credit card bill.

Bank: A financial institution that is licensed by the US government to make loans and take deposits. They're a safe place to store your cash because deposits are insured up to $250,000 per depositor.

Benchmarks: Steps or intervals you set on the path to your goals.

Billing cycle: The number of days between your last credit card statement and your current one. Usually around one month.

Bitcoin: A type of digital currency where new units of currency are created via the solution of complex mathematical problems. Can also refer to a unit of Bitcoin.

Bond: A loan you make to a corporation or government with your money. The company pays you interest for allowing them to use your money over a fixed period of time. Bonds are considered a more stable investment than stocks, but typically provide a lower return.

Bootcamp: A short but intense course of study to learn a particular technical or coding skill.

Brokerage firm/brokerage account: Companies that enable investors (like us!) to make trades in the stock market. When you open a brokerage account, that will be the account you use to buy and sell your investments.

Budget: A plan that outlines how you're going to use your money—a rundown of all the ways you're going to spend and save your money.

Business plan: A road map for your new venture that lays out what you're planning to do, how you think you'll make money and the obstacles in your way.

Capital: Money you use to start a company or keep it growing.

Career training program: A school that helps prepare you for a job in a particular field.

CD (Certificate of Deposit): A product you buy at a bank or credit union that pays a guaranteed rate of interest for keeping your money in that bank or credit union for a specific period of time (from three months to many years).

Check: Paper checks may seem like paying it old school, but this form of payment—which pulls money straight from your checking account—are still written about 16 billion times a year.

Checking account: A day-to-day transaction (i.e., spending) account with a checkbook and ATM card.

Clients: The people who pay for your services.

Co-insurance: A percentage of a medical bill that your health insurance requires you to pay.

Collateral: Property, cash, or other assets you promise to a lender in case you don't pay your loan. In the case of a car loan, the car is collateral. Credit cards, unless they are secured cards, don't have collateral.

Community college: A two-year college, sometimes called a junior college, where anyone can take classes at a reasonable price.

Compound interest: When you earn interest on your interest. It works behind the scenes to make your money grow without you having to do anything except make your first investment.

Consignment: Hiring another person or company to sell your belongings (like clothing or furniture) you no longer want. They pay you after the merch sells and keep a portion of the proceeds as a fee.

Co-pay: An amount you pay each time you see the doctor or get a prescription, in addition to your insurance premiums.

Co-signer: An additional person whose credit you are borrowing to secure your loan. If you don't pay your bill, your co-signer is on the hook.

Cover letter: A brief letter of introduction submitted with a resume that tells a little more about the applicant, their interest in the open position, and why they think they're good for the job.

Credit: The ability to borrow money from someone or something with the promise that you'll pay it back later.

Credit bureau: A company that collects information from creditors on how well you pay your bills, the types of debt you have, and how much of that debt you're actually using.

Credit card interest rates: The amount you pay the credit card company when you can't pay your bill in full every month.

Credit card: A payment tool issued by a bank, credit union, or other lender that lets you make purchases with borrowed money. If you don't pay off purchases in the month you make them, you pay interest.

Credit limit: The amount you're allowed to spend up to on a credit card. Spending up to your limit is called maxxing out. Hint: Don't do that.

Credit report: A written history of your bill-paying behavior. Do you pay on time? Go over your limits? Use credit excessively? Or not?

Credits: Payments that are credited to your bank account like your earnings from a paycheck, a birthday check from Grandma, or any other deposit you make.

Credit score: A financial grade that tells the companies lending you money how likely you are to pay your bills. It's shown as a number somewhere between zero and 850—the higher the better.

Credit union: A financial institution similar to a bank but owned by its members and operated not for profit but to benefit those members. Deposits are insured up to $250,000 per depositor so they're just as safe as banks.

Cryptocurrency: A digital asset secured by cryptography, making it nearly impossible to counterfeit. Many function via decentralized networks that run on blockchain technology. Cryptocurrencies generally operate independent of banking systems and governments.

Customers: The people who buy your products.

Debit card: A card tied to your checking account that allows you to make purchases or get money from an ATM.

Debits: Expenses, or the money you spend to buy things or pay down debt and rent. These are subtracted from your account balance.

Debt: Something—typically money—that you owe with a plan to pay it back later. You can have a small $5 debt to a friend or a $10,000 debt to a bank.

Deductible: The amount you're responsible for paying *before* your insurance kicks in.

Deferment (period): An agreed-upon time during which a loan does not need to be repaid.

Dependent: A person (often a child) who relies on others (like parents) for financial support and who can be claimed on someone's taxes as an exemption, which saves them money.

Depreciation: How much a car (or other asset) has dropped in value.

Direct deposit: Money moved straight from your employer/paycheck into your bank account.

Diversification: When all your investment eggs are not stuck in one basket. When your investments are diversified, you're less exposed to the ups and downs of any single company because you own many different stocks, bonds, or mutual funds.

Down payment: The amount you pay up front in order to drive off the lot with your car.

Endorse: Signing your name on the back of a check that is made out to you allows the bank to deposit it. You can also endorse a check over to another person to allow them to deposit it in their account by writing "Pay to the order of X person" and then signing your name.

Entrepreneur: Someone who starts and runs a business. People who start one business after another are called serial entrepreneurs.

ETF (exchange-traded fund): A mutual fund that follows a particular index but trades like a stock.

FAFSA: The Free Application for Federal Student Aid. It's a form you have to fill out before you apply to college in order to determine how much financial aid you'll qualify for.

Fast fashion: Low-cost clothing produced quickly, often overseas, in response to trends. It's a problem because a lot of clothing ends up in landfills, the industry is a big contributor to water pollution and the labor practices are often questionable.

Fed Funds rate: The interest rates banks and other financial institutions pay to borrow money overnight. When this rate goes up/down, banks raise/lower the amount they charge consumers to borrow and pay consumers to make deposits.

Federal income tax: Taxes based on the amount of earned income charged to individuals and businesses by the US government.

FICA: FICA stands for the Federal Insurance Contributions Act, and it's a tax you pay that will be taken out of your paychecks. Every time you pay into FICA, you're contributing to your Social Security benefits, which will be money you receive once you're retired. *See also*, payroll taxes.

Financial aid: A broad term that covers anything that helps you pay for college. Financial aid can be grants, scholarships, or student loans.

Financial plan: A road map that lays out your goals and the steps you need to take in order to get there.

Financial stress: Anxiety caused by money. Debt is a huge cause of financial stress.

Freelancer: Someone who makes money by finding clients to pay them for skills they have in a particular field.

Gap year: A year, typically between high school and college, used to travel, explore, and work.

Gender pay gap: The difference between what an average man is paid for a job and what an average woman is paid for that same job. Varies dramatically by race, sexuality, and disability.

Gift aid: Financial aid that doesn't have to be repaid. Grants and scholarships.

Gig worker: Someone who does tasks for other people—usually finding that work through apps or online platforms—and gets paid for it.

Goals: Things you have decided today that you want in the future for future you.

Grace period: The number of days after your billing cycles ends that you have to make payment. Typically 21 to 25.

Grants: Need-based financial aid given by state or federal sources that doesn't have to be repaid.

Health insurance: A just-in-case pool of money that you purchase in order to help pay your medical bills.

High-yield savings account: An online bank account that pays higher interest rates than traditional banks.

Identity theft: When your personal information is stolen and used to open fraudulent accounts or request a tax refund in your name.

Incentive: Different ways to make a car less expensive or put it on sale—from rebates (or money back) to 0% financing.

Independent contractor: A business owner who is hired by another business to do some work. Independent contractors are not likely to get benefits, but they have more freedom and flexibility over how and when they work.

Index fund: A type of mutual fund that contains only companies that are part of a particular stock market index (e.g., the Standard & Poor's 500, which is five hundred of the largest US companies; the NASDAQ index, dominated mainly by technology companies; etc.).

Inflation: Inflation is like a slow leak to your spending power. As time goes on, the price of things like homes, cars, college, coffee, and flip-flops rise.

Influencer: Someone with expertise or credibility in a particular area, who uses that clout to reach a big audience and then promote products, services, or brands.

Insurance: An arrangement or contract where you pay a smaller sum of money upfront to protect yourself against a higher cost due to loss of property or income, or illness down the road.

Interest: Money earned on deposits in savings accounts or paid in order to borrow money.

Internship: A job—sometimes paid, sometimes not—taken to gain experience in a particular career path or field.

Investing: When you put your money to work to make more money for you. You invest by putting the dollars you've already saved into something that grows over time, like a stock or a bond.

IRA: An individual retirement account that you can open through any brokerage firm and save money for future you.

Lease: A contract for the use of an apartment, a car, or another asset.

Lender: A company or institution (like a bank) that permits you to borrow money. When you take out a loan, you'll pay back your lender over time.

Loan: Borrowed money—student loans are for education, mortgages are for homes, auto loans are for cars—that you repay with interest.

Matching dollars: Money your employer kicks into your retirement account. Sometimes you have to contribute in order to get "matched," sometimes you don't.

Medicare: The government's health insurance program for people aged sixty-five or older. Some younger people with certain diseases and conditions may qualify.

Merit-based aid: Financial aid based upon your academic, athletic, or other achievements.

Military: The US armed forces, which offers training in many disciplines that can translate into careers. Also offers funding for post-military education.

Minimum wage: The smallest amount of money (usually per hour) that an employer can legally pay you to work for them.

Money Market Account: An account at a bank or credit union that pays interest on deposits. MMAs often pay higher interest rates than plain vanilla savings accounts but may have restrictions as well.

Mutual fund: A pool of many stocks, bonds, or other investments combined into a single investment in order to reduce risk.

Need-based aid: Financial aid based upon your ability to pay.

Needs: Things you must have for your survival, health, and overall well-being.

Negotiate: When you try to come to an agreement about something (like how much you'll be paid) by talking back and forth with another person or people.

Net (college) price: The amount college really costs after you subtract any grants and scholarships you receive.

Net income: Your pay after taxes and things like retirement contributions are subtracted.

Net worth: Someone's total wealth. Your net worth is calculated by adding all your assets then subtracting your debt. So if you have $5,000 in savings but you have $3,000 in student loans that you have to pay back, your net worth is $2,000.

Nonprofit organization: An organization that does not earn profits for company owners. Instead, profits go toward funding bigger organizational goals. Soup kitchens, churches, libraries, schools, universities, and credit unions are examples of nonprofit organizations.

Online bank: A bank without a storefront or other brick-and-mortar presence. These sometimes can offer higher interest rates on savings because they don't have to spend as much on real estate and staff.

Overdraft fee: A penalty you pay for spending more than you have in your checking account—typically $35, sometimes more.

Overdraft protection: Insurance from your bank that it will allow ATM and debit purchases to go through even if you don't have the money to cover them. You'll pay overdraft fees and sometimes interest on those transactions. If you don't have this, your purchase will be declined, but you won't pay needless fees.

Overdraw: When you spend more money than you have in your checking account.

Overspending: When we spend more than we earn or more than we have the ability to pay back. When someone goes into credit card debt, it's a sign they may have overspent.

Pay cycle: (Or pay period) This is how often you're paid by your employer, typically every two weeks.

Paycheck: Money you're paid for work completed. Paychecks used to be actual paper checks. Now many people have their pay directly deposited into bank accounts. Typically paychecks come every two weeks or twice a month.

Payment app: An app you can use to move money to and from your bank account (and credit cards) to pay friends and make purchases. Venmo, Zelle, and Paypal are all payment apps.

Payroll taxes: A portion of salary that is withheld from your paycheck and used to fund government programs including Medicare and Social Security. *See also,* FICA.

Pell Grant: A need-based form of financial aid that doesn't have to be repaid, given by the federal government.

Portfolio: The place where you put your investments. An investor's portfolio should contain a diversified mix of stocks, bonds, mutual funds, and other assets.

Premium: The monthly or annual fee paid for an insurance policy (health, auto, rental, etc.).

Principal: The original amount of your loan or deposit. If you borrow $5,000, that amount is your principal.

Pro/con list: A helpful way to make choices. You split your paper (or screen) in two and write down all the positives (pros) and the negatives (cons) associated with a given situation or choice you want to make.

Profit: The amount of money you make over what you spend on creating a product or service.

Racial wealth gap: The difference in the value of assets (homes, investments) owned by households in different racial or ethnic groups. Bigger than the gender pay gap.

Raise: When you increase your earning power by a certain amount. Sometimes your boss will reward your good work with a raise, but you'll often have to ask.

Rate of return: The amount you gain (or lose) on an investment over a particular period of time.

Rebate: Money you get back after making a purchase.

Renter's insurance: A type of property insurance that covers your belongings and provides liability protection, but doesn't cover the house or apartment itself.

Resume: A one-page document created by a person to present their background, skills, and accomplishments.

Retirement: When you leave your job and permanently stop working. Most people decide to retire at age sixty-five or over.

Rider: An add-on insurance policy that provides protection for valuables (art, technology, jewelry) not covered under your homeowner's or renter's insurance.

Risk: The possibility—which varies—of losing money on particular investments.

Risk appetite: The amount of risk you're "hungry" for or the amount of risk you're willing to take with your money.

Room and board: The cost of a place to live and meal plan while at school.

Roth IRA: Another type of IRA into which you can invest no more than $6,000 per year. You can pull the money out without penalty to buy your first house or pay for school if you need to.

Salary range: The range of pay you're willing to accept from an employer. For example, you can say you'd like to earn between $15 and $20 per hour for a job.

Savings account: An account that earns interest and where you keep money you're saving for short-term or long-term goals.

Scholarship: Merit-based financial aid, given from a variety of sources, that doesn't have to be repaid.

Secured credit card: A credit card that requires a small deposit down in order to get the card and establish your credit limit. This card is like credit card "training wheels" to help you build credit.

Security deposit: Additional money you pay at the beginning of a lease that can be used to cover damage to the property when you leave. If there is no damage, you should get this money back.

Self-employed: A full- or part-time worker who contracts with other people to get paid for their work. For example, a doctor or lawyer with her own office is self-employed. Someone with a food truck is self-employed, as is a yoga instructor or dog walker.

Shareholder: Someone who owns stock in a company.

Social Security: This is the term used for the Old-Age, Survivors, and Disability Insurance (OASDI) program in the United States, which is run by the Social Security Administration (SSA), a federal agency. It provides retirement benefits, survivor benefits, and disability income.

Socially responsible investing (SRI): Investing in companies that line up with your beliefs.

State income tax: Taxes charged based on the amount of income you earned while living or working in a particular state. Some states have no income taxes.

Stock: A small slice of a company's business. When you buy stock in a company, you become a part owner of that business.

Student loans: Borrowed money that you have to pay back with interest. There are two main types of student loans: federal student loans and private student loans.

Subsidized (loans): These do not accrue (or add) interest while you're enrolled in school or during deferment periods.

Target-date fund: A mutual fund designed to grow money to be used at a particular date in the future (usually for retirement).

Term: The amount of time until a bond matures or repays your principal.

Ticker symbol: A unique set of letters used to identify a stock for trading purposes.

Title: Legal proof that you have a right to (or ownership of) a property like a home or car.

Total compensation: The full amount you are paid to do a job, including not just your salary but benefits like health insurance, retirement contributions, and vacation time.

Trade school: A school that teaches students skills needed for a technical career

Transfer program: Two years of study at a community college before moving to a four-year school to get a bachelor's degree.

Treasury Bill (T-Bill): Issued by the US Treasury, this is a short-term investment with a maturity period of up to one year (fifty-two weeks).

Tuition: The cost of classes or a course of study.

University: A higher-education school that typically offers both undergraduate and graduate degrees and conducts a lot of research.

Wants: Things you'd like to have, but would be just fine without.

Withholding: Taxes deducted (i.e., withheld) from your paycheck and sent to the government. You want to withhold enough so you don't have a big tax bill but not so much that you're giving the government an interest-free loan.

Working papers: "Working papers" is the common term for a Certificate of Age Form, which is a document that teens need in order to work. These papers show that you meet the minimum age requirement to be hired, and certify that you can be employed.

Yield: The interest you earn on your bond.

SELECTED SOURCES

"Annual Credit Report.Com." 2021. annualcreditreport.com/index.action.

Cautero, Rachel Morgan. "How Much Does Routine Car Maintenance Cost?" April 16, 2021. thebalance.com/average-car-maintenance-cost-4775765.

"Compound Interest Calculator." moneygeek.com/compound-interest-calculator.

Connley, Courtney. "These Are the 20 Best Jobs in America in 2020, According to a New Ranking—and They're Hiring." January 15, 2020. cnbc.com/2020/01/15/the-20-best-jobs -in-america-in-2020-according-to-glassdoor-ranking.html.

"Facts + Statistics: Identity Theft and Cybercrime." iii.org/fact-statistic/facts-statistics-identity -theft-and-cybercrime.

Folger, Jean. "Investing in Index Funds: What You Need to Know." June 11, 2020. investopedia .com/investing-in-index-funds-4771002.

Gravier, Elizabeth. "Living in These 9 States Means You Don't Pay Income Tax, But Here's What to Watch Out For." March 29, 2021. cnbc.com/select/states-with-no-income-tax.

Horymski, Chris. "People Are Going into Debt for Rewards Points and Miles: Survey." June 27, 2018. comparecards.com/blog/rewards-card-debt-survey.

"Learn More, Earn More: Education Leads to Higher Wages, Lower Unemployment." May 2020. bls.gov/careeroutlook/2020/data-on-display/education-pays.htm.

"Number Of Jobs, Labor Market Experience, Marital Status, And Health: Results From A National Longitudinal Survey." August 31, 2021. www.bls.gov/news.release/pdf/nlsoy.pdf

"Occupational Outlook Handbook: U.S. Bureau of Labor Statistics." bls.gov/ooh.

"Range of Returns for Three Major Asset Classes." 2021. fc.standardandpoors.com/ondemand /public/products/chartsource/chart.vm?topic=5899&siteContent=8221.

Sandoiu, Ana. "Financial Worries May Raise Heart Attack Risk by 13-Fold." November 11, 2017. medicalnewstoday.com/articles/320037.

Twiddale, Alaina. "If You Still Don't Believe in The Power Of Compound Interest, You Have to See This." May 17, 2021. moneyunder30.com/power-of-compound-interest.

Torpey, Elka and Dalton Terrell. "Should I Get a Master's Degree?" September 2015. www.bls .gov/careeroutlook/2015/article/should-i-get-a-masters-degree.htm#Masters%20box.

iNDEX

JEAN CHATZKY is the CEO and co-founder of HerMoney, the author of thirteen books, an award-winning magazine columnist, and the host of the *HerMoney* podcast. After decades of reporting on personal finance—including twenty-five years on *The Today Show*—she knows that now more than ever, a successful financial life is within every woman's grasp—and with the HerMoney team, she's on a mission to help you get it. In her free time, Jean loves running, finding new ways to use her sourdough starter, and cooking for friends. Raised in the midwest, she now lives in Philadelphia with her family and new pup. Find her @JeanChatzky on Twitter and Instagram.

KATHRYN TUGGLE is the chief content officer and Gracie Award–winning editor in chief at HerMoney.com. She produces the *HerMoney* podcast and co-hosts its popular mailbag segment. Originally from Birmingham, Alabama, Kathryn has spent the last two decades in New York writing and editing for magazines, television, and websites. When she's not educating women about their money, Kathryn can probably be found thrift store shopping, teaching a yoga class, or browsing bookstores in Paris. Find her @KathrynTuggle on Twitter, Instagram, and TikTok.

HERMONEY is an inclusive digital media company focused on improving the relationships women have with money. We're on a mission to level the playing field for financial security and power by providing financial coaching and educating our community on: how to know what fair pay is and how to ask for it, how to invest and grow wealth, how to talk to our friends and family about money, how to use our voices to create change, and so much more. With our website, weekly newsletters, and *HerMoney* podcast, we provide judgement-free information that's more than just numbers. Because when you understand money, you gain confidence and freedom, which is exactly what we want for everyone reading this book. We can't wait to have you as part of our community at HerMoney.com and on Twitter and Instagram @HerMoneyMedia.

NiNA COSFORD is a freelance illustrator based in the UK. Her work mostly focuses on storytelling—particularly female-centric themes—and has amassed a global audience of over 350,000 followers. She has illustrated over twenty published books and has collaborated with numerous brands including Apple, HBO, WaterAid, TATE, Google, and Netflix. She also loves to travel and draw her way around the world—recording people, places, and cultures in her sketchbook wherever she goes. Find her @NinaCosford on Twitter and Instagram.